on track ...

Ralph McTell

every album, every song

Paul O. Jenkins

Foreword by Ralph McTell

SONICBOND

sonicbondpublishing.com

Sonicbond Publishing Limited
www.sonicbondpublishing.co.uk
Email: info@sonicbondpublishing.co.uk

First Published in the United Kingdom 2023
First Published in the United States 2023

British Library Cataloguing in Publication Data:
A Catalogue record for this book is available from the British Library

ISBN 978-1-78952-294-5

Typeset in ITC Garamond Std & ITC Avant Garde Gothic
Printed and bound in England

Graphic design and typesetting: Full Moon Media

Permission to use excerpted lyrics from 'Streets Of London' and 'The Ferryman' was granted by TRO/Essex Music Group. All other lyrics used by permission of Leola Music Ltd. Permissions to use album cover images were granted by BMG and Leola.

Follow us on social media:
Twitter: https://twitter.com/SonicbondP
Instagram: www.instagram.com/sonicbondpublishing_/
Facebook: www.facebook.com/SonicbondPublishing/

Linktree QR code:

on track ...

Ralph McTell

every album, every song

Paul O. Jenkins

Foreword by Ralph McTell

SONICBOND

sonicbondpublishing.com

Dedicated to the memory of John Beresford

Prelude: Haiku for Ralph

Abandoned son writes
Songs for the brotherhood of
Those he never knew.

Author's Acknowledgements

I owe great thanks to a good many. Besides being a good friend, Andy Langran has assembled a wonderfully informative and comprehensive Ralph McTell website (Ralph, Albert & Sydney www.ralph-mctell.co.uk) that I mined repeatedly. In a sense, this book gives flesh to the skeleton Andy has created.

Over the years, I have benefitted greatly from the wisdom of fellow McTell fans. These include Marianne James, John Thompson, Domenico Mosca and countless others.

Roger Federer, Rod Laver, Kevin DeBruyne, Matt LeTissier, James Ward-Prowse and Ian 'Chico' Hamilton provided artistic inspiration.

My entire family, especially my brother, Hugh, sister Carol, my mother, Barbara, and my wife, Mary, lent emotional support. Oldest brother and poet, Clay, lent valuable advice in regard to lyrics. Over the years, I have delighted in 'watching love grow' in the context of my son, Tom.

Ralph May himself has always been willing to respond to my gushing fan letters and frequent questions.

Brantley Palmer, Luke Newman and Courtney MacKinnon helped with image scanning.

The interlibrary loan staff of DiPietro Library at Franklin Pierce University (Jill Wixom, Amy Horton and Melissa Robbins) were invaluable to my research.

Melinda Jette helped with translations of some passages in French. Special thanks are due to my editor at Sonic Bond Publishing, Stephen Lambe, as well as his entire staff.

Stuart Ongley played a key role in helping to obtain permissions. Ralph McTell's son, Tom May, and daughter, Leah, were both very helpful in a number of ways.

Foreword

It was the guitar that led me to write songs, and before that, it was the harmonica or mouth harp (that all small boys seemed to own in the fifties) that introduced me to making music. Somewhere in between harmonica and guitar came the piano and the orchestral polyphony that came from it and continues to fill me with wonder.

From an early age, poems and narrative stories amazed, delighted, and frightened me by turn. Song lyrics had profound meaning for me even before the work of American writers reached me. At school in the morning assembly, our glorious hymn tunes often moved me to tears.

Growing up in the UK, we were limited to one or two radio stations playing very light popular songs, but hearing my mother sing lyrics of war-time melodies probably had just as much effect on my later writings as Woody Guthrie or Bob Dylan. My songs have 'weathered in time's wilderness', and I hope they have matured in the airing of performance. I am very happy that songs I wrote 50 or more years ago still get requested.

This book examines in great detail the songs themselves but it is important to stress that the guitar has often been the stimulus to write the lyric. I imagine most songwriters concentrate on melody first. However, the melody is often the last part of writing to arrive.

If I have a subject in mind, the first priority is mood. This itself usually dictates the tempo and whether the song should be in a major or minor key. Next come chord shapes and voicing. Then, because I play mainly fingerstyle, I use my thumb to address the possibility of a simple bass line against the strings used in the chord. In my more recent work, I often think of the subject first and then commence to write the lyric and find the melody nestling in the accompaniment, which is waiting within the guitar arrangement. I work mainly in the top four frets of the guitar and I do not read music.

Tunings, voicing, bass lines and emerging melodies that beg words to accompany them have very often suggested the subject that will become the lyric. I work just as hard on those criteria as on a song's lyric and have even included some guitar arrangements as stand-alone instrumentals on the album *Sofa Noodlin'*. These 'rules' may well have limited my song output, but if the song has been recorded, then it will have had to pass this test.

My desire is to communicate my views of life and experience through songs, and this continues to be my driver. Live performance is vital to my whole sense of well-being. I have now reached a place where I realise this is what I have done with my life, and I am very fortunate to be in a position where I enjoy sharing the experience more than ever.

I love my job and have no plans to stop writing and working. I will continue to aim at the standard that Paul has been gracious enough to commend. I find his observations honest, perceptive and fair. This is his book, and I feel honoured that he considers me worthy of this academic analysis and forensic research; I have both learned and benefitted from it.

Thanks, Paul!

Ralph McTell, February 2023

on track ...

Ralph McTell

Contents

From Croydon to Here: Significant Dates in the Life and Career of Ralph McTell

We know a great deal about Ralph McTell. He has written two volumes of his autobiography (*Angel Laughter* and *Summer Lightning*), released a three-CD set (*As Far As I Can Tell*) of recordings from talks based on those volumes, given numerous candid interviews and was the subject of an excellent study (*Streets Of London: The Official Biography Of Ralph McTell*) by Chris Hockenhull in 1997. While it goes without saying that every artist draws on their life experiences for material, McTell's work is so heavily informed by events in his life that it is useful here to include a condensed overview of the man and his career. In *Summer Lightning*, McTell writes: 'Most of my songwriting is autobiographical. The incidents described in them have become songs because it has been possible to contain the poetry or symmetry within the confines of the song format'.

1944: Ralph May (he will later take the stage name of McTell) was born on 3 December in Farnborough, Kent. May's father, Frank, named his son after his one-time employer, Ralph Vaughan Williams. Before the war, Frank worked in domestic service, first as a chauffeur and later as a gardener, before becoming a car mechanic once he left the army. Ralph's mother, Winifred Iris Moss, was also in the service and was 28 when her son was born.

1946: McTell's brother, Bruce May, was born. He would play an important role in McTell's career, serving as his manager for many years.

1947: McTell's father abandoned his family to live with another woman. In shock, Winifred struggled to hold her young family together, scrubbing doorsteps and taking in ironing to make ends meet. Eventually, the family settled in Croydon, a borough of London, and moved into a damp basement apartment. McTell's mother later found work in a chemist's shop.

1949: In February, McTell suffered life-threatening wounds, hit by flying glass, when a drunken lorry driver drove into a shop window near the pavement where McTell and a friend were looking into a sweetshop window. He spent 15 weeks in the hospital, often attended by an Irish nurse named Mary. Upon his release, he convalesced with his grandparents in rural Brackley (Oxfordshire).

Circa 1950: McTell saw his father for the last time. It was another traumatic incident in his life and he recalled it vividly. He flew into a rage, vowing to take care of his mother. McTell (*Angel Laughter*, 45): 'Suddenly I burst out with a string of invective that stopped both my parents in their tracks and they just turned and stared at me'. McTell (Hockenhull, 9): 'The feeling of needing a father figure to look up to stayed very close to me until my late teens'. McTell eventually found such a man in his upstairs neighbour, Kevin Connaughton, whom he would later pay tribute to in song.

1951: McTell began playing harmonica after receiving the instrument from Kennards, a department store in Croydon. McTell was a popular child, full of invention and high spirits despite the challenges with which he had been presented.

1952: On 2 November, 16-year-old Christopher Craig shot and killed a police officer in Croydon. His accomplice, Derek Bentley, was later executed for the crime. The injustice of Bentley's death stayed with McTell his entire life and prompted him to portray the incident in song years later.

1957: Frank May was electrocuted in an accident. Despite his anger at his father, young McTell was devastated. McTell (Grenfell, 81): 'I just could not cope. But I also could not cope because I always nurtured the thought that I would get to see my dad one day and find out what went wrong'. The May family moved house to 17a Miller Road. McTell enrolled in the John Ruskin Grammar School to prepare for the eventual admission to university. He was terribly unhappy there, however, feeling 'outclassed' by his more affluent peers and talked his way into being demoted from form 3U to the less stressful 2W. He learned to play the ukulele and formed his first band, whose repertoire included songs by Lonnie Donegan and Buddy Holly.

1960: Unhappy at school and hoping to finally 'belong to something with a structure to it', McTell decided to join the Junior Leaders Battalion of the Queen's Surrey regiment. He was miserable in service, though, and after six months, borrowed £50 from his mother so she could 'buy him out'. As part of the arrangement, McTell resumed his schooling at Croydon Technical College, promising to pursue some O-levels, but his heart was not in it. He eventually received an A level in Art. In a move that would change his life forever, he took up the guitar. His inspiration was an EP by Ramblin' Jack Elliott called *Muleskinners* that included a cover of Jesse Fuller's 'San Francisco Bay Blues'. Dozens of American country blues artists soon began to crowd his imagination. His first guitar, acquired from Kennards, was barely playable, but its promise was still seductive.

1960-1965: McTell's years of wandering and apprenticeship. At Croydon Technical College, he met like-minded students and embraced Beatnik culture. McTell began to learn the guitar in earnest with the help of Max Faulkner. Weekend trips to music festivals became frequent, and he started to seriously consider a career as a performer. He sharpened his craft by briefly joining the Hickory Nuts, an English bluegrass band that featured

Pete Chalkey on banjo, Ray Tassey on mandolin, and Mick Lewis on double bass, before making a tentative start as a solo performer. Still shy and lacking confidence, he was helped greatly by Wizz Jones, an established and respected folk artist. In 1961, he visited the continent for the first time, busking in Munich and Paris. McTell also embarked on his first serious romantic relationship and the couple travelled to Spain together. He hitchhiked throughout Europe, visiting Belgium, Italy, Germany, Greece and Turkey with a succession of friends and musical mentors, including an American, Gary Petersen, who notably improved the young performer's guitar techniques and helped him expand his repertoire. While in Paris in 1965, McTell met and quickly fell in love with Nanna Stein, a Norwegian woman working there as an au pair.

1966: McTell returned to England after a lengthy spell in Paris and considered moving to America. Upon learning that Nanna was pregnant, the couple married in Norway on 30 November. They subsequently moved in with McTell's mother in Croydon, before relocating to Cornwall. McTell was now writing his own songs and briefly joined a jug band fronted by Michael Bartlett, aka Henry VIII. McTell then began to tour (mainly in Cornwall) with Wizz Jones. Upon seeing his name paired with Jones' on posters advertising their gigs, the young performer felt it didn't sound quite right. He would prefer a last name that included two syllables. He had long delighted in the music of the blues performer Blind Willie McTell and suggested rechristening himself as a performer by the name of Ralph McTell. Jones concurred, and the stage name was thereafter used. Some of McTell's live performances from this period are included in his box set, *The Journey*, released in 2006. On stage, McTell now included some original compositions to augment the folk and blues covers that still dominated his set lists.

1967: McTell and his wife moved back to London with their son, Sam, born on 21 January. McTell was still undecided as to his eventual career choice. He studied for a year at a teacher training college in Tooting before finally deciding to become a full-time performer. He became a fixture at Les Cousins in Soho, joined Essex Music as a house writer and soon signed a recording contract with Transatlantic, the then-top UK folk label under the direction of Nat Joseph.

1968: McTell's first LP, *Eight Frames A Second*, was released to favourable reviews. He met double bass player Danny Thompson, who would become a staple on future recordings. Bruce May became his older brother's manager.

1969: McTell's second album, *Spiral Staircase*, was released. Producer Gus Dudgeon, convinced a reluctant McTell to include a track he had been working on since 1966. It was called 'Streets of London'. On 24 August,

McTell performed the song on BBC's 'Country Meets Folk' program. Hundreds of listeners called in to learn the identity of its performer. Later the same year, McTell's third album, *My Side Of Your Window*, appeared. Its strongest track was 'Michael in the Garden', loosely based on Nanna's autistic brother, Olebjorn.

1970: McTell's star continued to rise. His live performances attracted the attention of ambitious American entrepreneur Jo Lustig, who became the young performer's new manager. Due to his increasing reputation as a composer, McTell was now known more as a singer-songwriter than simply as a 'folkie' and Lustig felt eager to introduce his star to a larger audience. McTell was immediately apprehensive about such a move, presciently stating (Hockenhull 54): 'I don't want to be a big star, because I'd end up a nervous wreck; I'm much happier playing in the more intimate and friendly atmosphere of a small club'. Emblematic of his growing stature was McTell's performance on 30 August, at the three-day Isle of Wight Festival, which featured folk legends like Joan Baez and Richie Havens, along with rock stars Jimi Hendrix and The Who.

1971: McTell's second child, Leah Hannah May, was born on 9 February. Eager to expand his audience, McTell played some dates in the United States. The title track of his new album, *You Well Meaning Brought Me Here*, reflected McTell's growing uneasiness with the pressures of the profession. Another important song, 'The Ferryman', was a lengthy treatment of many of the dilemmas that confront those who have chosen an artist's life.

1972: *Not Till Tomorrow* was McTell's first album for his new label, Warner Bros. It was successful and captured the sound McTell had long been looking for but was not the popular breakthrough Lustig or Warner Bros. was hoping for. Tensions mounted between McTell and his manager. They agreed to part ways and Bruce May resumed his role as manager.

1973: McTell played to a full house in London's Royal Albert Hall.

1974: McTell's new album, *Easy*, was his first LP to chart, reaching number 30. As the Christmas season neared, Bruce May suggested that 'Streets of London' should be re-released as a single. It reached number two in the charts and immediately spawned a multitude of cover versions. The song's success forever changed not only McTell's career but also his life. In the era of Glam Rock acts such as David Bowie, Mott the Hoople and Roxy Music, the track's simplicity, compassion and eloquence lent it a certain distinction. Long popular with both concert attendees and radio listeners, the song had already appeared in Capitol Radio's list of All-Time Top 100 singles, even though it had only recently been released as a single. The modest McTell seemed almost embarrassed by its success and was certainly uncomfortable to have a hit on his hands.

1975: Eager to capitalise on the unexpected hit single, Warner Bros. convinced the reluctant McTell to include the song on his next album, titled simply, *Streets*. It became the former folkie's biggest chart success, reaching number 13. The tour arranged to further maximise the new star's success proved fraught with complications, however. McTell did not always include the hit single in his set list, which prompted negative reactions from new fans who had bought tickets primarily to hear it. The band McTell assembled failed to jell on stage and frustrations mounted for the newly famous performer. 'Since I've had a hit record', he stated (Hockenhull 84), 'life has become a misery. I keep getting hustled into doing things I don't want to do and I'm losing the respect that I had for myself'. In the spring, McTell fled to Los Angeles by himself, desperate to get his head together. He considered abandoning the stage and devoting his time strictly to the studio as The Beatles had done a decade earlier. A new single, 'Dreams of You', based on Bach's 'Jesu, Joy of Man's Desiring', was a modest success, reaching number 48 in the singles charts, but McTell 'never really believed in the song' and turned down an opportunity to perform it on *Top Of The Pops*.

1976: A second son, Tom, was born on 7 September. McTell again sold out the Royal Albert Hall. Eager to try something new, he decided to work with American producer Shel Talmy, best known for his numerous hits with The Kinks. Though the goal was to create an album that would have greater appeal to an American audience, the sessions produced a collection of songs that sounded more like middle-of-the-road country western than Ralph McTell. Unreleased until 2022, when it saw the light of day on various internet listening services under the title *Tequila Sunset*, its songs included a combination of lesser McTell originals (with the exception of the excellent title track) and country western staples like 'I Fall To Pieces' and 'Abilene'. Much more successful was *Right Side Up*, released the same year, which included two of McTell's best songs, 'Naomi', and 'From Clare To Here'.

1977: McTell toured Australia for the second year in a row, playing to large and enthusiastic audiences. A live album, *Ralph, Albert & Sydney*, was released that contained tracks from his 1976 tour in the Land Down Under combined with those from a performance at the Royal Albert Hall.

1978: Billy May was born on 19 April.

1979: McTell played a few dates on the east coast of the United States, including a memorable set with Bert Jansch in Boston. Recorded with many of his Fairport Convention pals, his latest album, *Slide Away The Screen*, was released.

1980: Out of contract with Warner Bros., McTell and his brother Bruce founded their own label, Mays Records.

1981: McTell joined forces with Richard Thompson, Dave Pegg and Dave Mattacks to form The GPs (short for Grazed Pontiffs), a short-lived 'super group'.

1982: *Water Of Dreams* was released in the autumn. It featured a number of protest songs, including 'Bentley and Craig' and the title track.

1983: McTell agreed to appear as co-host for a Granada TV children's series, *Alphabet Zoo*. It proved popular and McTell released an accompanying album of songs.

1984: McTell hosted a second Granada series, *Tickle On The Tum*. He embarked on a brief US tour.

1985: Still wracked with self-doubt and unsure of what direction his career should take, McTell reluctantly agreed to record a series of pop standards. The resulting album, *At The End Of A Perfect Day*, pleased no one, least of all McTell.

1987: *Bridge Of Sighs*, his first collection of original songs for adults in four years, appeared. Very much a comeback album, it featured a host of excellent compositions, including 'The Setting', 'The Girl From The Hiring Fair' and 'Mr. Connaughton'.

McTell opened for the Everly Brothers on their UK show dates.

1988: Suffering from writer's block, McTell released a collection of acoustic blues covers, *Blue Skies Black Heroes*. He explained (Hockenhull 119) that 'recording those tunes was a way of acknowledging my debt to those people and my wish is that it will turn people onto that music and they too will go on and develop an interest in it, as happened with me'.

1990: *Stealin' Back*, a second collection of blues covers, was released.

1992: *Saturday Rolling Round*, an album by the GPs, appeared. Inspired by reading a biography of the Welsh poet Dylan Thomas, McTell awoke from his creative slumber in the form of *The Boy With A Note, An Evocation Of The Life Of Dylan Thomas In Words And Music*. Ten original songs were augmented by 11 spoken word 'investigations' that served to explore the true nature of the fabled bard.

1993: McTell toured Australia and the Far East.

1995: Another strong collection of original songs, *Sand In Your Shoes*, appeared. If McTell was not now as prolific as in his youth, his compositions displayed the wisdom of an artist who has fully learned his craft.

1996: McTell contributed to *Billy Connolly's World Tour Of Australia* television series.

1997: Chris Hockenhull's biography of McTell, *Streets Of London*, was published.

2000: *Red Sky* was released. 18 of the lengthy album's 19 tracks were originals, including the strongest songs, 'In The Dreamtime' and 'Easter Lilies'. McTell's first volume of his autobiography, *Angel Laughter*, was published.

2002: McTell released *National Treasure*, an album of covers. *Summer Lightning*, the second volume of his autobiography, appeared. He was awarded a Lifetime Achievement Award for Songwriting at the annual BBC Radio 2 Folk Awards.

2004: McTell celebrated his 60th birthday with a sell-out concert at The Royal Festival Hall. He toured Australia, Ireland and continental Europe.

2005: *Time's Poems*, a collection of McTell's original lyrics, was published.

2006: *Gates Of Eden*, a collection of songs by musical heroes Woody Guthrie and Bob Dylan, was released. *The Journey*, a three-CD box set retrospective accompanied by two essays about McTell's music, also appeared.

2010: *Somewhere Down The Road*, McTell's first collection of original songs in ten years, was released to positive reviews.

2014: McTell performed at the Royal Albert Hall in honour of his 70th birthday.

2016: *About Time*, a relaxed and enjoyable album of covers played with old friend Wizz Jones, appeared.

2017: *About Time, Too*, a second collection of songs performed with Jones, was released.

2019: *Hill Of Beans*, a strong album of original compositions, was released.

Introduction

Like all composers whose work is destined to outlive them, Ralph McTell knows that one key to artistic longevity is the ability to tell a good story. If many of his tales stem from personal concerns, even more are universal in appeal. Most of us, after all, have known an 'Old Brown Dog', reminisced about the 'Barges' of our childhood, sought comfort in a 'Tequila Sunset', or sought reconciliation on a 'Bridge of Sighs'.

Yet if McTell excels at crafting such narratives, he is perhaps even more skilled as a portraitist. His compositions are populated by a fascinating cast of characters. Over the years, his listeners meet, among others, the pious Mrs Adlam, the determined Alexei, the hopeful Factory Girl, the faithful Geordie, the lonely Doreen, the sceptical Claudia, the poetic Sylvia, the loyal Naomi, the skilful Joseph, the needy Martin, the friendly Mr Connaughton, the defiant Michael, the doomed Otto Schwarzkopf, the helpful Harry, the joyous Maddy, the self-pitying Rosalinda, the decisive Reverend Thunder, the repulsive Puggy Mearns, the mysterious Arthur Blake, the intriguing Bad Girl and the sagacious Ferryman.

But the more we become familiar with his work, the more we begin to suspect that, endearing as these figures might be, the most intriguing character of them all is McTell himself. While his sketches of figures, both historic and imagined, are impressive, those songs I characterise as McTell's self-portraits are notable not only for their candour but also for their lack of conceit. As a songwriter, McTell is able to somehow gain the necessary distance and perspective to treat his own life as he might that of any other. A man of great talent and compassion, McTell's most telling characteristic is his honesty. If he is honest with his listeners, he is still more candid with himself, readily sharing the kind of insecurities that plague the less gifted among us. It is rather ironic that an artist so willing to write about his own experiences with true candour should have chosen to rebrand himself via a pseudonym. To my mind, there is far more May than McTell in the work he has left us.

McTell's father abandoned his family when Ralph was still quite young and this trauma, coupled with a life-threatening accident that befell him as he unsuspectingly walked down a Croydon pavement, left its mark on the man. Referring to the kinds of ups and downs we all experience, McTell has admitted to Michael Grenfell, author of an excellent 2016 study of the songwriter, that he is 'never level' (23), adding that he is 'still very soft and sensitive' (17). Even with his impressive catalogue, McTell has often harboured a sense of self-doubt. In an interview with the author (20 December 2022), he compared his work with that of peers like Al Stewart, Bert Jansch, Roy Harper and John Martyn, explaining that while those performers seemed to play with an enviable certainty, he lacked a similar conviction. 'I seek to instil empathy in my listeners. My songs pose questions rather than make statements'.

And yet, guided by the simple principle of trying to please others by expressing himself to the best of his abilities, McTell has left us with a significant legacy. If he does not always highly regard himself, McTell has often been recognised by others, winning the Ivor Novello award (best song musically and lyrically) in 1975 for 'Streets of London', as well as the BBC Lifetime Achievement Award for Songwriting in 2003.

A well-read man, McTell bases his informal rules for songwriting on American novelist John Steinbeck's guidelines for writing a good story. (Memory is a tricky thing, of course. Steinbeck actually devised six rules for writing a novel and they differ from what McTell remembers). First, each song should contain at least one truly original line; second, the melody should be memorable; third, the accompaniment should be interesting; fourth, the lyrics should be as poetic as possible; and finally, the song should be governed by the notion that brevity is the soul of wit. McTell has admitted that he sometimes struggles with this last tenet. The fact that so many of McTell's songs meet these criteria is a testament to his abilities and to his preference for what he calls 'traditional' songwriting. McTell (Awde 193): 'I like proper songs in proper formats... And I tend to move towards more the conventional structures in songwriting because I can evaluate them better and appreciate them because they tick all the boxes that I feel are as important in my own life'. Creating new work can be quite a painstaking task for him. As he told Andrew Means in an interview for *Melody Maker* (29 August 1970): 'You wouldn't believe how long I spend on the lyrics of songs. I sometimes take ages trying to decide between two incredibly simple words. I am really pleased if people listen to my words because the tunes are really a vehicle for the lyrics'. He goes on to downplay the significance of his work, concluding that his hope is to craft pieces of universal appeal.

> I don't have a message as such. I didn't start writing songs because I had an idea of how to change the world or knew the answer to Man's problems. The most rewarding thing is when people come up after hearing me play and say that they feel the same way as my songs. Really, our emotional responses are the same. I am beginning to write songs about how I am actually feeling right now, but most of them are still about how we all feel.

If McTell's most important contribution to popular music is his compositions, one should also note both his sensitive guitar work and his expressive baritone voice. Interestingly, McTell does not fancy himself much of a singer, preferring to call himself a guitar player who sings. Yet the unaffected expressiveness of his voice is one of the secrets to his success. He loves the country blues and excels at emulating the ragtime guitar stylings of Blind Blake in his covers, while also producing intriguing instrumentals of his own, like 'That'll Do Babe' and 'Willoughby's Farm'. As he told Nick Awde (197): 'I have learnt to play in a rather muscular way considering I play fingerstyle.

I'm blessed with very strong fingernails and I thumb pick, so my bass end on the guitar is always very strong... I think those early days when there were no mics in the clubs sort of forged my style'. McTell has stated that he is continually amazed at the variety the instrument offers. Often, he will start the process of composition by finding a chord that suggests a certain mood. He will then stitch on another chord until he begins to find his way. The finger-picked accompaniments he creates are similar to those of James Taylor, a contemporary to whom he has sometimes been compared and whom McTell very much admires. Besides their skills at composing thoughtful songs, Taylor and McTell alike are capable of not simply singing a piece but caressing it, due both to their sensibilities and the smoothness of their voices. I find McTell has a more pronounced edge to him than Taylor, however. This is especially evident in his protest songs, a genre Taylor doesn't explore in anywhere near the same depth ('Millworker' representing an exception).

While acknowledging that his 1974 hit, 'Streets of London', was central to his career, McTell often felt burdened by the unrealistic expectations it produced. Arlo Guthrie, the son of McTell's idol, faced a similar dilemma. After rising to fame through his lengthy spoken diatribe, 'Alice's Restaurant Massacree', Guthrie was pressured to come up with a follow-up hit and become something he never aspired to be: a folk-rock star. Still, another contemporary whose work is similar in some ways to McTell's is Al Stewart. Both Stewart and McTell are literate writers who began as 'folkies' before moving into the world of folk-rock. After having established firm fan bases, both artists expanded their listenership by composing hit singles, 'Streets of London' and 'Year of the Cat'. Both performers then struggled with the pressure exerted upon them by their labels to create further hits. Stewart was more successful in this regard than McTell, following 'Year of the Cat' with 'Song on the Radio' and 'Time Passages' before, like McTell, returning to relative pop obscurity while maintaining his original fan base.

Both Stewart and McTell thus enjoyed a period of chart popularity that eluded talented colleagues like Bert Jansch (1943-2011), John Renbourn (1944-2015) and Davey Graham (1940-2008). Each of these influential guitar players was important and retained large followings, but none 'broke through' with radio hits as Stewart and McTell did. Another key distinction is that Jansch, Renbourn and Graham never sought such popularity. Neither, in fact, did McTell. His struggles with the pressures of fame are well documented and he has often stated that he never sought the adulation that came with having a hit record. McTell (Awde 183): 'I've flirted and tried to make it more commercial and radio-friendly and stuff like that and it's been a total waste of time because it's not helped, it's actually hindered'.

Before embarking on our exploration of McTell's substantial body of work, it is useful to provide some statistics in order to establish the scope of his achievement. He has written approximately 300 original compositions and included more than 350 songs on the 26 major albums he has released to date. Of the 138 original compositions written for adults that I have identified as having a distinct theme, about 40% concern love, 13% treat concerns unique to those who create art, 10% are protest songs, 8% are instrumentals and 7% treat the wonders and challenges of childhood. The remaining 22% deal with optimism, loneliness, religious faith, fathers, history and compassion. At the conclusion of my study, I have included some suggested thematic playlists that reflect some of these breakdowns.

This short book catalogues the songwriter's contributions to our world, album by album, track by track. Writing about music is difficult, and has, in fact, been compared to 'dancing about architecture' (a quotation attributed to many down the years, from Martin Mull to Elvis Costello). In my analysis, I generally concentrate on McTell's lyrics, only mentioning the musical accompaniment he uses when it significantly augments the piece. I have also, in a sense, played favourites. Particular compositions stand out in every artist's career and McTell's is no exception. I have thus chosen to devote more attention to a few of his most important songs and trust that the reader will understand the reasons for more detailed analysis and discussion. After treating the 16 albums that include largely original material, I make a less detailed study of those that chiefly feature covers, were recorded in concert, or are compilations of previously recorded tracks. Due to necessary space limitations, I am unable to expand on all of his artistry or treat his children's material, but I hope that readers new to McTell will be inspired to explore his recordings and that those long familiar with his songs will glean some new insights and be inspired to listen anew. Ralph McTell's work is evergreen and rewards its listeners with visions of 'bright and beautiful things', while simultaneously providing the resolve to weather whatever storms may await them in darker times.

Noted author Louis de Bernières, best known for the bestselling *Corelli's Mandolin*, named his 2015 novel, *The Dust That Falls From Dreams* after a line from McTell's 'Walk Into The Morning' (*Somewhere Down The Road*). On the album's liner notes, de Bernières writes: 'No one else can write songs of such warmth. I have loved his work for 30 years and it has become as much a part of myself as Bob Dylan's has'. I particularly appreciate de Bernières' mention of McTell's 'warmth'. It was this quality that initially drew me to McTell and one that sets him apart from others who are otherwise equally skilled.

Finally, in a work that treats more than 300 songs, it is inevitable that factual errors will appear and I acknowledge my responsibility for each and every one of them.

Eight Frames A Second (1968)

Personnel:
Ralph McTell: guitar, vocals, harmonica
Mac McGann: double-neck guitar
Mick 'Henry VIII' Bartlett: jug
'Whispering' Mick Bennett: washboard
Bob Strawbridge: mandolin
Recorded at Pye Recording Studios, October 1967.
Produced by Gus Dudgeon.
UK release date: 1968.
US release date: 1969.
Highest chart places: did not chart.
Running time: 38:54

Like many debut albums, *Eight Frames A Second* is inconsistent. This is due in part to the fact that it was the inaugural effort not only for McTell but also for its producer, Gus Dudgeon (1942-2002). Though Dudgeon would later go on to produce Elton John and David Bowie, in 1967, he had more experience as an engineer. Arranger Toni Visconti (b. 1944), was also a neophyte at this early date and some of his work sounds a bit heavy-handed and at odds with the material. McTell describes Dudgeon (Awde, 197) as a 'fantastic producer, but he wanted everything to have sparkling clean underwear', adding that he 'had total control over the final mix'. While acknowledging that Dudgeon 'made some brilliant records' later in his career, he feels his approach failed to capture the essence of what McTell was trying to achieve in these early recordings: 'one bloke and a guitar'. The young performer felt Dudgeon was working under misguided instructions to try to make him a crossover pop star.

Recorded for Transatlantic, a label that would eventually include top folk acts such as John Renbourn, Bert Jansch, John Fahey, Billy Connolly and The Dubliners, *Eight Frames* serves as an accurate representation of McTell's emerging sound. Covers of blues standards were still a major part of his live repertoire and are on full display here. While some of its eight originals are merely competent, others like 'Nanna's Song', 'I'm Sorry I Must Leave' and the title track suggest a promising future and an already established gift for both lyrics and melody. Nat Joseph was greatly impressed by Leonard Cohen and asked McTell to record 'Suzanne' during the sessions. Since McTell was dissatisfied with the results, the recording was not included on the original release. This track, along with 'Boodle Am Shake', Jesse Fuller's 'San Francisco Bay Blues' and 'I Love My Baby' are included on the CD release of the album.

Considering how unfamiliar most record buyers would have been with McTell in 1967, the fact that the cover does not include his name is rather unusual. Bobby Davidson's cover photo shows a rather drawn-looking McTell gazing into the distance. Though McTell found it a bit posh, a quotation from

Robert Browning's poem, 'Fra Lippo Lippi', is included on the back cover: 'paint the soul. Never mind the legs and arms'. Its inclusion here is a reminder of what is truly important to good art in any form. On his first collection, McTell's soul is front and centre. We recognise him as a compassionate, thoughtful man who has much to offer his listeners. The unusual phrase used for the album title refers to slow motion and McTell's perception of light as it slowly appeared and illuminated the clubs he played in.

Eight Frames A Second sold well for a debut and would eventually earn a gold disc in 2004.

'Nanna's Song' (McTell)

A lovely way to lead off McTell's debut album and one of the first pieces he ever wrote, 'Nanna's Song' is a moving portrait of his courtship of the Norwegian woman who would later become his wife. McTell still remembers where he first saw her: outside a bar at the end of the Rue des Écoles in Paris, sporting a Leslie Caron haircut, wearing a green coat and black suede boots. While the song's details are personal, its sentiments are universal. McTell immediately establishes an intimacy with his listener through his soothing voice and sensitive guitar work. While a tone of innocence pervades the piece, it is nevertheless indicative of a songwriter who is ready for his first close-up. As in many of his pieces, McTell includes here a reference to dreams and their relationship to the real world, where time, like a river, swiftly passes by. Time itself plays a major role in the song. Like many young people, McTell wants to freeze the moment and hold onto this emerging moment of love in all its splendour. He is, of course, aware of the impossibility of this desire, but is nevertheless in its thrall. The intermittent guitar fills extend the reverie. The chimes of Notre Dame pick up the insistent nature of time, while the transition from romantic evening to prosaic morning is already feared. It is a strong testament to McTell's precocity that he could have written such a wise song at such an early age; that while still in love's first blush, he could stop to realise that even the strength of young love is no match for Father Time. In his preoccupation with time, we see one reason McTell would later grow so fond of Dylan Thomas, one aware, even as a youth, that time held him 'green and dying', though he sang in his chains like the sea.

'The Mermaid And The Seagull' (McTell)

This fanciful bit of whimsy reminds one of some of Donovan's early compositions. A product of the composer's enchantment with Cornwall, its dream-like feel places it firmly in 1968. The song features various shifts during its four-minute running time and portrays a theme of misrepresentation. While the first two verses are firmly planted in reality, the last three are pure fancy. Beer-drunk, money spent and ignored by passersby, the narrator is obviously ready for a change. He finds one in two new companions, the title characters, and is eager to please them. Four of the five verses end with a farewell of sorts, indicating that even reveries are temporary.

'Hesitation Blues' (Traditional, arranged by McTell)
McTell's cover of this oft-recorded blues piece demonstrates his familiarity and comfort with the genre. He is most at home with such covers that are a bit light-hearted. The song is most often associated with the Reverend Gary Davis. McTell delights in relating how he once had the opportunity to perform another of Davis' songs, 'Death Don't Have No Mercy', in person for the great man, only for the legend to state that he didn't recognise it.

'Are You Receiving Me' (McTell)
This is a rather minor contribution to the album that humorously details how the best of intentions can go astray. The narrator fails to connect with each of the characters he encounters. The song's awkward meter is indicative of the inconsistency of McTell's early original work.

'Morning Dew' (Dobson)
Though the song is attributed to Tim Rose (1940-2002) on the LP, it was written by Canadian folkie Bonnie Dobson (b. 1940), who recorded it in 1962. Rose's 1967 folk-rock cover of the piece was briefly in vogue, perhaps explaining the misrepresentation. Its angst-ridden lyrics portray the fears of a couple living in what we presume is a post-apocalyptic world devastated by nuclear weapons. Though he liked the song a great deal, McTell doesn't sound fully at ease in his cover version, perhaps reflecting the fact that he knew two popular versions of the song already existed and that he was contractually obligated to include it on the album. Shortly after McTell covered her tune, Dobson returned the favour, recording McTell's 'Clown' in 1969 and 'Factory Girl' in 1970.

'Sleepy Time Blues' (McTell)
This slow, bluesy original is a self-admonition to behave better sooner so as to avoid later regrets. It resembles a lullaby in some ways, with the distinction that the narrator is trying to sing himself to sleep rather than another younger party. One of his first attempts at composition, McTell recalls writing it in a caravan park in Penzance one rainy day.

'Eight Frames A Second' (McTell)
McTell (Hockenhull, 45): 'The title track is about the dawn and how light shades and colours change and that it happens every day'. It is in essence, a tribute to Eos, the Greco-Roman world's personification of dawn. The unusual topic of the song demonstrates young McTell's ambitions. Even at this stage of his career, he is not content to merely write love songs or explore his personal feelings. Rather sombre in tone, the track features poetic lyrics

that are overwhelmed at times by Visconti's string arrangements. McTell has jokingly sworn that no drugs were used in the making of the song.

'Willoughby's Farm' (McTell)
A lovely, bucolic instrumental that demonstrates McTell's considerable finger-picking prowess on the guitar. The bridge in the middle of the piece and its conclusion are both inventive.

'Louise' (McTell)
This earnest, energetic original features a jug band sound, a Robert Johnson-style guitar introduction and numerous tempo changes. Though well executed, the composition feels a bit constrained by the tradition that inspired it and features blues conventions rather than displaying the sort of lyrical gift McTell had earlier demonstrated in the title track.

'Blind Blake's Rag' (Traditional, arranged by McTell)
Blind Blake (aka Arthur Blake or Arthur Phelps) was an important early influence on McTell. Throughout his career, in fact, McTell recorded far more Blake songs than those of his adopted namesake, Blind Willie McTell. 'The effect of this man's music on me was enormous', McTell writes in his liner notes to his 1988 *Blue Skies Black Heroes* album. 'I have never heard anyone who came close to his ability'. This amalgam of blues numbers demonstrates that Blake's admirer has considerable ability himself. Such ragtime pieces were an important part of McTell's early repertoire and endeared him to listeners in clubs where he performed.

'I'm Sorry I Must Leave' (McTell)
This tightly structured song employs an unusual A/A/A/B rhyme scheme and begins each verse with a subjunctive 'if' clause. The lover is doing his best to be honest in this breakup; to continue as things are, he explains, would be wrong. Though he is the one initiating the breakup, he assures his lover that the pain is not limited to her. Many of McTell's young listeners could surely relate to this all too common predicament.

'Too Tight' (Blake)
McTell's second homage to Blind Blake on the album is a faithful cover of his 1927 original.

'Granny Takes A Trip' (Bowyer/Beard)
A novelty song originally written and recorded by the Purple Gang as a homage to a Chelsea boutique, 'Granny' is an odd choice to end McTell's debut album. While he was obligated to record it as part of his record deal, it might have been given a less prominent place here. Still, it's difficult to generate much anger towards such a raucous and high-spirited number.

McTell was considerably relieved that the track didn't take off with listeners, thus avoiding being regarded as a performer of novelty pieces.

Spiral Staircase (1969)

Personnel:
Ralph McTell: guitar, vocals, harmonica
Brian Brocklehurst: double bass on 'Last Train And Ride' and 'Spiral Staircase'
Mick 'Henry VIII' Bartlett: jug on 'Last Train And Ride' and 'Spiral Staircase'
Mick Bennett: washboard on 'Last Train And Ride' and 'Spiral Staircase'
Peter Berryman: guitar on 'Last Train And Ride' and 'Spiral Staircase'
Produced at Regent Sound Studios by Gus Dudgeon
UK release date: 1969
Highest chart places: did not chart
Running time: 35:27

McTell's second album is far stronger than his first. Two covers and two instrumentals serve to leaven the 'heavy' nine originals, which include stand-out compositions, 'Streets of London', 'England 1914', 'Daddy's Here', 'Terminus' and the title track. There's a certain haunted feeling that pervades the entire album. This is the work of a thoughtful young man with a great deal on his mind. McTell rises admirably to the task, showing a deft hand as he deals with historical, fictional and personal topics, and his vocals sound newly assured. Producer Gus Dudgeon, seems more comfortable with his task than he had with *Eight Frames A Second* and lends suitable tonal background to such a complex set of lyrical themes. To top things off, an old friend from McTell's time at Croydon Art College, Peter Thaine, contributes a fascinating cover design that, besides featuring a spiral staircase, includes archaic typography, a small portrait of a guitarist ascending to new heights and a plethora of curlicues and Celtic knots. The album holds up well to repeated listening and earned gold disc status in 2004.

Richie Unterberger's brief review for *Allmusic.com* praises some numbers ('England, 1914' and 'The Fairground') while finding others merely 'OK', including McTell's reading of 'Kind Hearted Woman Blues', which he deems 'least memorable'. He describes the album as 'low key and wistful'.

'Streets Of London' (McTell)

McTell's second album opens with his most famous song. He was unsure of the piece, originally offering it to another artist (who found it 'too sad') and had to be convinced by Dudgeon to include it. While it's easy to understand its great popularity over the years, the composer doesn't rate it as highly as some others in his canon in terms of quality. The chorus, with its direct and challenging question, is the strongest part of the song and makes it feel personal to every listener. On four separate occasions, we are asked:

> How can you tell me you're lonely
> And say for you that the sun don't shine?
> Let me take you by the hand

> And lead you through the streets of London.
> I'll show you something to make you change your mind.

Self-pity is a vice we all fall prey to. Yet, after hearing this song, it is one we never quite experience the same way again. The verses, also phrased as questions, are not as powerful as the chorus, but include wonderful details that bring to life the old street people who are the focus of the song. Our mind's eye sinks to the streets as we picture the old man 'kicking up the paper with his worn-out shoes'. He is a discard, still awake while others sleep, as seemingly irrelevant as 'yesterday's news'. Later, the old man ruminates over a cup of tea, but wisely McTell does not give us a glimpse into the nature of his thoughts. We feel we already know their tenor, so further exposition is unnecessary and would be clumsy. The final verse, composed years after the song originated in 1966, may be the saddest of all, yet it holds a promise for a better world. As long as such pieces are written – and find such a receptive audience – perhaps there is hope for 'a world that doesn't care'.

McTell has spoken at length about the song's genesis (Hockenhull, 140). He wanted to write something for his friend, Martin 'Tubs' Sole, who had fallen on hard times.

> It was just a tune initially. I put a few chords together, but nothing really happened, then I got C, G, A minor, E minor, F and C, and when I got that sequence, it became a tune almost immediately. What particularly pleased me was that the bass line was there from the start, so basically, it almost wrote itself. The verse stayed with me for some time, but the middle eight came quite a while later.

Like many of his songs, it was informed by personal experiences. McTell (Hockenhull, 141):

> I used images from my childhood of Surrey Street Market in Croydon. There was this one guy who used to go around after the market had closed for the day looking for fruit and vegetables that had fallen off the stall onto the floor. He wasn't at all embarrassed and used to kick around the waste paper, almost pretending to be unconcerned. What struck me was that he appeared to be most uninhibited in his scavenging.

As a teenager, McTell experienced an incident that led to the song's second verse. One day, a lone woman began to move towards him (Hockenhull, 141-42):

> She was one of the bag ladies. She was shuffling towards me with all these bags that obviously contained her worldly possessions. It always struck

> me as odd that the men never seemed to carry very much with them, if at all, but the women did for some reason. I looked around and there was no one else on the street. As she came towards me, I felt in my pockets and gathered what loose change I had with me. As she passed, I didn't say anything but dropped the coins into one of her bags and carried on walking past. I'd only walked a few feet when I heard her shout and I turned around. She'd put her bags down, removed the coins from them and hurled them back at me, yelling 'I don't want your effing money' and other abuse. It startled me. I had meant it as a simple act of kindness – I'd never patronise these people. In the first verse, I included the line, 'In his eyes you see no pride', but she did have her pride. This woman obviously wanted her independence and not charity.

Then, later, McTell explains the line that includes mention of a teacup (Hockenhull, 142): 'The teacup is their horizon line for all they have in the world. The line "looking at the world over the rim of his teacup" is to say that he can't see anything in the world beyond the rim of the cup he holds'.

The composition's final verse was written months after the others (Hockenhull, 142-43):

> At the bottom of Factory Lane was a hostel occupied by all sorts of men: labourers, drop-outs, some who were quite disturbed and so on. This one old guy was a First World War veteran and he used to wear slippers all the time along with a homburg and an old greatcoat with his army medals on. As a young boy, he used to frighten me when I saw him.

Listeners immediately embraced the song. Cover versions began to appear weeks after its release, and to date, it has been recorded by more than 200 performers. Some of McTell's favourite interpretations include those by Sinead O'Connor, Mary Hopkin and Harry Belafonte, whom he once heard speak rather than sing the lyrics in performance. He feels the song is most effective when delivered by youthful performers. One of the most unusual covers was by the English punk band Anti-Nowhere League, in 1982. Obviously more raucous than other interpretations, it also included some altered lyrics, such as, 'I'll show you some things you'll never understand' and 'I'll show you some things that will make you really sick'.

If the song has often had a profound effect on its listeners, McTell himself was stunned by how listeners at the Cambridge Folk Festival in the late sixties reacted to it. McTell (Hockenhull, 143):

> I really didn't have any idea how well my career was going in those days, because the interest in me hadn't really hit home. I felt it had died a death the first time I ever performed it in public – there was this split-second silence at the end that seemed an eternity. I suppose it transports people

> somewhere as they hear it and at Cambridge, the whole crowd sang along with it, which was totally unexpected – I felt a lump in my throat. Martin Carthy came up to me as I came off stage and couldn't believe the impact the song had made. I was stunned.

The song has remained popular and seems destined to qualify as an evergreen tune. A new recording featuring McTell and former Eurythmics vocalist Annie Lennox, was released as a charity single in December 2017. In March 2020, McTell agreed to write another verse, inspired by the COVID-19 pandemic gripping the world at the time.

> In shop doorways, under bridges, in all our towns and cities
> You can glimpse the makeshift bedding from the corner of your eye
> Remember what you're seeing barely hides a human being
> We're all in this together, brother, sister, you and I.

A charity named Streets of London has been established with McTell as one of its ambassadors. To date, the organisation has raised more than £750,000 to aid London's homeless population. Both as a piece of art and a conscience-provoking catalyst for positive change, 'Streets of London' has had a tremendous impact on the world. Though, for a time, he wearied of feeling obligated to perform it every time he took the stage, McTell remains (Hockenhull 145) 'immensely proud of the song. It is certainly not the best song I've ever written, but if you seek to touch hearts and move people, then it succeeds from that point of view'. In an email (28 November 2022) to the author, McTell adds that the song 'undoubtedly changed my life'.

'Mrs. Adlam's Angels' (McTell)

This composition is a detached but affectionate look back at McTell's old Sunday school days. His own teacher there was actually a Mr McKay, but he felt the song would benefit from the alliteration resulting from the use of the name of his brother's teacher, Mrs Adlam. McTell (interview with the author, 20 December 2022): 'I was moral, I was a good kid. I believed all that stuff. But I had serious doubts about angels'. The song is nostalgic and descriptive; the adult McTell, no longer a believer, passes no judgment on the old lady. Indeed, Sundays at her house are described as a 'dream' and McTell makes it clear that her intentions were to reassure the children that the angels would protect them. The piece ends with the mature narrator wondering if such child-like faith is even possible anymore. The echo of T.S. Eliot's famous verb 'dare' here is playful but also indicative of McTell's ongoing struggle with the attractions and contradictions of faith. McTell (Awde 176): 'I think there's always been a need for a spiritual sort of recognition. And when it was taken away by my growing maturity and realisation that there probably wasn't a God, then I felt that music fills that void for me – it's probably man's highest art'. In *Angel Laughter* (30), McTell simply states: 'Of course, I saw angels, but they afforded me scant comfort'. Throughout his early childhood, McTell also heard voices inside his head. *Angel Laughter* (36): 'I suppose I became used to hearing the voices... I convinced myself on more than one occasion that God had spoken to me through my mind and advised me to become a missionary in far-off lands'. At times, however, the voices inside his head were more sinister, 'muttering and murmuring in tones of discontent' (*Angel Laughter*, 37). It was only years later, when McTell discovered the joys of music, that these internal demons ceased their din.

'Wino And The Mouse' (McTell)
A brief, whimsical instrumental that breaks the contemplative mood created by the previous track. In *Summer Lightning* (309), McTell recounts his inspiration: 'This little old man used to sit outside the self-service restaurant on St. Germain des Prés on a piece of cardboard. He played little meandering notes on a penny whistle whilst a little mouse ran up and down the length of the instrument in an appearance of dancing'.

'England 1914' (McTell)
McTell (Hockenhull, 47): 'The song is a premonition of disaster and despair and destruction and the way it would be from then on. Never before had men had the power to destroy themselves quite so comprehensively. The song's about that and the sadness at England's loss of naivety –its rural phase. I'm not talking about Victorian values but the loss of peacefulness'. One of McTell's most powerful early compositions, it shows his ability to treat serious, even profound, topics with a poet's touch. Even though Mike Vickers' well-intentioned string arrangement rather overwhelms the lyrics, the glockenspiel provides a nice element and the listener delights in the composer's varied and poignant imagery. In a song that is ultimately about the destructiveness of war, McTell cunningly chooses to include everyday details instead of settling for more obvious and trite representations. When he composed the work, McTell was unaware of the following passage written in the 1925 memoir of British foreign secretary Sir Edward Grey, which is quite similar to the piece: 'It was getting dusk, and the lamps were being lit in the space below on which we were looking. My friend recalls that I remarked with the words: "The lamps are going out all over Europe, we shall not see them lit again in our lifetime"'.

'Last Train And Ride' (McTell)
McTell again changes the album's mood, offering the listener a song that shows how blues can be playful. A marked improvement over the original blues numbers included in his first collection, lines, such as the one that references the Heinz condiment, prove that we are dealing with a songwriter who looks to surprise his listeners instead of merely treating them to tired

clichés. McTell's guitar gets in on the act, too, offering the listener numerous aural winks throughout the piece. The addition of sarcastically sombre backing vocals completes the delight.

'The Fairground' (McTell)
An interesting exercise in juxtaposition, this song asks which is more real: the fantastic fairground, full of movement and magic, or the more prosaic and stagnant daily world. In some ways, then, it recalls 'The Mermaid And The Seagull' from McTell's previous album. The narrator gradually concludes that however seductive the fairground may be, he must 'get off the ride' and return to a more mundane existence. He achieves self-forgiveness in this realisation, however. The candy stick messages, previously unclear, become plain in the last verse. There is great variety here in almost every sense: tempo changes, bridges and tone. The song's accompaniment is as ambitious as the lyric, but both arranger Mike Vickers, and producer Dudgeon, rise to the occasion, taking the listener on a ride sprinkled with appropriate musical magic. McTell's vocals find greater range than normal here, and if they sound a bit stilted at times, the listener appreciates the variety.

'Spiral Staircase' (McTell)
Another song that features motion, the album's title track is a bit reminiscent of Bob Dylan's 1962 single, 'Mixed Up Confusion'. McTell himself described the work as illustrating 'an up-tempo dilemma' where true progress is difficult to achieve and perplexed uncertainty results. The narrator reaches no resolution in the song. At its beginning, the staircase is winning and by its conclusion, it is aflame. Staircases, of course, imply upward motion, but here it is likened to a drill and the listener is aware that upward mobility, in the sense of McTell's ever more successful career, can be as frightening as it is enthralling. The clever lyrics are nicely joined to the kind of ragtime guitar accompaniment so beloved by the composer.

'Kind Hearted Woman Blues' (Johnson)
A gentle version of the Robert Johnson standard that has been covered by dozens of artists. McTell's guitar work is fine and his harmonica solo shows his dexterity on the instrument. After hearing the originals on the album, this return to a blues written by another composer sounds a bit jarring and out of place.

'Bright And Beautiful Things' (McTell)
An odd, and even chilling, variation on the proverb, 'big fish eat little fish'. The gentle tone of the music is quite at odds with the starkness of the lyrics. The insertion of McTell's rhetorical question, 'oh, who do you blame', is poignant. A brief instrumental inclusion of the hymn, 'All Things Bright And Beautiful', nicely underscores the theme of hypocrisy McTell explores here.

'Daddy's Here' (McTell)

Told in the first person and played in a slow, wistful way, this song effectively expresses a child's anxiety that accompanies the increasingly rare visits of his father. Touchingly, the child's first thought is about the effect the visit will have on his mother. The child appreciates how his father's desertion has unnerved his mother, the stable, remaining parent, and the source of badly needed security. Such compassion is a McTell trademark. On the other hand, in the third verse, the stable mother leaves the boy and his brother alone in order to speak in private with her husband, prompting fresh anxiety in her sons. McTell's use of atmospheric detail in the song is excellent. Mirroring the boy's anxiety is the dying sunshine he sees on the walls and the growling dog he hears in the hall. The anxious children are reduced to trying to guess what the latest twist in the plot of their lives will be. Worth noting, too, is the fact that the artist in the boy/McTell is already present. To ease their fears, the boy and his brother tell each other stories. Soon enough, however, order is restored to their lives. The everyday, comforting details of 'radio, celery and Sunday tea' signal a return to normalcy. Life is better without the interloping father and somehow, the boy knows that he will no longer disrupt their domestic stability. The song's title is key. Even as he composed it, McTell's father was present; he was 'here'. Naming the piece 'Daddy's Home', for instance, would lend it an entirely different tone. 'Home' no longer includes the father. Considering the anger McTell has felt over the years for his father, the song is remarkably gentle and has a beautiful melody and accompaniment. Perhaps the young narrator's knowledge that 'he won't come again' lends him some reassurance and peace. Though McTell never forgave his father for deserting the family, in the first volume of his autobiography, *Angel Laughter*, he finds some explanations – if not justifications – for Frank May's sometimes violent behaviour. During his relatively short life, May suffered a nervous breakdown, spent time in prison, occasionally slept rough and generally never seemed to find much satisfaction in life.

'Rizraklaru' (McTell)

The odd title of this instrumental is an anagram of 'rural karzi', Cockney slang for a privy. McTell relates that it was inspired by Mick Bartlett's 'musical accompaniment to his ablutions'. Having read the genesis of the short piece, listeners may be unprepared for the fact that it is peaceful, gentle and lovely.

'(My) Baby Keeps Staying Out All Night Long' (Moss)

Here, McTell reworks Buddy Moss' 1933 song, 'Daddy Don't Care'. This version is much more up-tempo than the original and McTell makes numerous changes to the original lyrics, including the fact that the narrator does, in fact, mind very much that his baby is keeping odd hours, something that the original addresses more indirectly.

'Terminus' (McTell)

'Terminus' is an appropriate closing number for the album and succinctly describes a moment of separation. The song begins with a transitory word, 'finally', and paints the end of a picture that has been a work in progress for some time now. It portrays the power of love, its ability to derail plans, mute voices, still thoughts and even stop time. In the second verse, McTell catalogues the lovers' sensations, noting their sore eyes, sweetly aching bodies and cold feet. Whether this last image is meant to evoke a possible cause of their separation or is merely accidental, it is yet a telling detail. The third verse returns attention to feet, as a gentle force of nature – in the form of a playful wind blowing paper past their feet – is contrasted with the shrill whistle of a train. The latter is a harsh reminder of the reality of their situation and robs them of 'the last seconds' they are trying to make the most of. The narrator is left to muse alone in the song's final two verses. The outside world continues its intrusions, this time in the form of a stranger asking for a light. Thus, the motif of the intrusion of real life upon reveries already seen in 'Fairground' and 'The Mermaid And The Seagull' again appears. By the final verse, the narrator has achieved enough perspective to realise his situation is far from unique, that on another platform, 'the same old scene is to be shot again'. The wind returns at the song's end, picking up more paper (just as it does in 'Streets Of London') and the narrator leaves to travel with the zephyr, perhaps now as free as this elemental force. McTell will revisit the scene later in his career with 'The Setting'. Vickers' string arrangement is restrained enough not to distract the listener from such a touching lyric.

My Side Of Your Window (1969)

Personnel:
Ralph McTell: guitar, vocals, harmonica, piano
Bruce Barthol: bass
Neil Cawley: flute on 'Michael In The Garden'
Brian Brocklehurst: bass
Gary Petersen: guitar, piano on 'Girl On A Bicycle', organ on 'I've Thought About It'
Phil Greenberg: guitar
John Marshall: drums on 'I've Thought About It'
Clive Palmer: banjo, fiddle on 'Blues In More Than 12 Bars'
Mick Bennett: percussion on 'Blues In More Than 12 Bars'
Folk Weavers: backing vocals on 'Kew Gardens'
Produced at Regent Sound Studio by Ralph McTell
UK release date: 1969
Highest chart places: did not chart
Running time: 37:27

His first collection to feature all original compositions, McTell's third album shows a maturing artist increasingly concerned with personal and societal issues. 'Clown', 'I've Thought About It' and 'Wait Until The Snow' exemplify the former, while 'Michael In The Garden', 'Father Forgive Them', 'Factory Girl' and 'Blues In More Than 12 Bars' treat topics of broader concern. The album's title, of course, underlines this dichotomy. Here, McTell also takes on the role of producer and the results are encouraging. Though he admits to sometimes having been 'seduced' by the possibilities that string arrangements could bring to his songs, his approach is controlled and tasteful. Always a sensitive man, McTell had grown worried that listeners might have come to regard him as 'soft'. It was his hope that pieces like 'Michael In The Garden', 'I've Thought About It' and 'Blues In More Than 12 Bars' might reassure his audience that he was able to pair steel with silk. Though the album is generally strong, a few missteps appear. 'I've Thought About It' and 'All Things Change' sound dated to this listener's ears and some find 'Kew Gardens' a bit too precious.

Robin Denslow's liner notes cast McTell as 'a born outsider trying to come to terms with it all through his music', and the songs presented here indeed portray numerous individuals trying to fit into a society that is not always accepting of 'the other'. Peter Thaine's rather Victorian cover art portrays three characters from the LP, including a girl on a bicycle.

'Michael In The Garden' (McTell)

McTell leads off the album with one of his strongest compositions to date. The composer has characterised it as the kind of song one can only write when young. He has also written, in his 1972 songbook, that it 'is not autobiographical, though there have been times when I wished it were'. It is a personal work, however, having been inspired by Nanna's brother, Olebjorn. The song is awkwardly structured and must have been terribly difficult to sing. It's also noteworthy that McTell, the artful finger picker, strums the piece. This departure adds to its power immeasurably. In a sense, then, the performance reflects the very differentness of Michael's world. Structured more straightforwardly, the message may have come off as jejune. After three standard verses with a chorus, in which those outside Michael's world are referred to as 'they', the song veers off into a first bridge that changes the comparison from Michael/they to Michael/we. This is a very clever shift on McTell's part. Whereas early in the piece, the listener has joined with McTell in their condemnation of others, they are now forced into self-examination. The second, longer bridge heaps line upon line, heightening the tension in Dylan-esque fashion until we win release and gain resolution just as Michael does. The fact that McTell places Michael in a garden is also, of course, significant. Michael is the pure boy in the garden, a spot long associated with innocence. Indeed, garden imagery occurs throughout McTell's work ('Kew Gardens', 'Peppers And Tomatoes', 'Genesis Chapter 1 Verse 20', 'Jesus Wept', to name a few). By contrast, the outside world's experience and wisdom are captured in the imagery of a spider web that traps both ourselves and Michael, here compared to a butterfly. If the innocent Michael is able to pardon us, McTell's attack on conventional wisdom is far less forgiving. The composer has written that the piece has generated nearly as much correspondence as 'Streets Of London', with many of the letters coming from parents of children who have faced similar challenges.

'Clown' (McTell)

One of the composer's favourite songs on the album, 'Clown' can be read either literally (as a circus performer's lament) or as a metaphor for the artist's lot. Many a performer would understand the clown's realisation that much of his own identity is tied to his show business persona. Yet again, the real world and the world of imagination and reverie are contrasted, as are children with adults, innocence with experience. Light imagery joins the two worlds in the final verse, suggesting a possible bridge and a happy ending. This prospect is reinforced by the song concluding with the image of the clown laughing at the night. If the laughter may still be tinged with bitterness, it is laughter nonetheless. The track's musical accompaniment begins conventionally, but McTell's harmonica signals a tempo change midway through the piece.

'Girl On A Bicycle' (McTell/Petersen)

The American guitarist Gary Petersen co-wrote this song with McTell and plays on the track. In *Summer Lightning* (311-312), McTell recounts the first time he heard Petersen play his Martin D-28 as a young man in Paris. 'Amongst my friends, I was regarded as a pretty good guitarist, but in Gary's company, I was a rank beginner. His classical ragtime playing was sensational;

my jaw literally dropped at the things he could do and it stayed dropped'. Petersen became one of McTell's musical mentors. 'Each day, I was learning something new. I was discovering new harmonies and my right hand was beginning to master the mind-over-matter techniques required to play ragtime properly'. Just as the big wheels spun on 'The Fairground', so the girl's bicycle wheels spin around here, even when the bike has stopped moving. The trees near the river move as well before also ceasing at the song's conclusion, one of many comparisons between the girl and the natural world made in the piece. Twice the sun flashes in the young rider's hair. Quite where all this is going eludes this listener, but a coherent message is less important than the song's lovely dreamlike feel. A gentle string arrangement and Petersen's soft piano complement the guitar accompaniment. This atmospheric tune gained radio play in Holland and Germany when covered by Dutch singer-songwriter Herman van Veen, under the title 'Fiets' (Dutch for bicycle).

'Father Forgive Them' (McTell)

According to McTell's biographer, Chris Hockenhull, this song was recorded for (but never included in) a film named *Staircase* that was designed to portray a more compassionate view of homosexuality than was typical of the time. And although the line that mentions that Jesus kept the company of men becomes clearer in this context, the song is really general enough to be a condemnation of nearly anything or anybody that runs counter to middle-class values. Just as he would later come to the defence of travellers in 'Gypsy' and 'Pykey Boy', here, the young McTell asks for more sympathy for those considered 'outsiders' by the straight population. His choice of the first-person plural saves the song from sounding too sanctimonious. The last line includes the recognition that all of us, no matter our sexual orientation, must ask God for forgiveness. McTell's vocal approach is atypically aggressive at times, while the use of reverb sometimes lends a feel of monastic chants to the recording.

'All Things Change' (McTell)

McTell rates this work as one of his most poetic early compositions and has stated that it still moves him to this day. In some ways, an attempt at an art song, 'All Things Change' pairs ambitious lyrics with an adventurous string arrangement by Tony Visconti, and McTell features on piano for the first time on record. If the song sounds a bit awkward and forced at times, poetic touches, such as the snails' 'tinseled trails' and the impermanent nature of the lovers' breathy promises, are indicative of the writer's emerging gifts. McTell rerecorded the piece many years later for his *As Far As I Can Tell* album and has stated that he prefers that less adorned version.

'I've Thought About It' (McTell)

'I've Thought About It' is an example of one type of protest song, as identified by American sociologist R. Serge Denisoff, in that it identifies conflict or discontent in a society, usually in emotional terms. It is very straightforward and relies heavily on McTell's impassioned singing and playing. There are no grey areas in the song; things are either good or bad, a belief typical to people not yet fully attuned to life's complexities. Unlike his inclusive choice of the first-person plural in 'Father Forgive Them', McTell here uses an 'I' and 'they' approach. The overall effect of the song is thus a bit self-righteous. Still, there are some nice touches, such as the sly organ insertion in the fifth verse that mentions Jesus.

'Factory Girl' (McTell)
This song is a tender and compassionate look at the routine, often monotonous existence of a young woman, confined by workplace walls and economic station, but ever hopeful of some change that will release her. If the preceding track was pessimistic, here McTell's strain of optimism is present. Despite her soul-sucking employment, the girl has 'joy in her eyes', and even in an urban setting, she is able to find consolation in the natural world in the form of a songbird. The song thus provides an excellent example of McTell's skill as a storyteller, demonstrating an ability to identify small details and build his portrayal around them. The flute contributions in the bridge foreshadow the bird song and lift the piece, just as the young girl's spirits are lifted by the sounds of nature.

'Blues In More Than 12 Bars' (McTell)
Unlike 'I've Thought About It', this playful romp demonstrates that songs with a message need not be deadly serious in tone. Set to a jaunty tune, it's the story of Billy, a young ne'er-do-well who eventually rises to power by learning the nature of the game in a society rife with corruption. After landing in jail a number of times, Billy gets wise, gaining the kind of knowledge that enables him to become, in turn, mayor, governor and, finally, President of the United States. Setting the song in America lessens its sting for the UK audience and fits well with the playful, bluesy nature of the music. The addition of Clive Palmer's banjo and fiddle, along with Mick Bennett's percussion, helps to make this a protest song that the listener enjoys rather than endures.

'Kew Gardens' (McTell)
Although he later acknowledged that he had never visited the spot at the time of writing, McTell chooses the historic Kew Gardens as the setting for a brief romantic encounter. The young lovers made famous by the French cartoonist Raymond Peynet (1908-1999), helped to inspire the song. The writer enjoys internal rhyming and the technique is certainly on display here (cool/pool, hazy/lazy, here/there, warm/lawn, scented/blended, linger/finger, etc.). McTell deftly employs a bridge as the turning point in this rather sentimental song that avoids a saccharine conclusion when the two lovers are parted,

not united. Mary Hopkin, who would later marry producer Tony Visconti, recorded it for her 1971 *Earth Song, Ocean Song* album.

'Wait Until The Snow' (McTell)
This is a strong track with a timeless feel that explores a common human desire: the wish to run away from problems rather than face them. In some ways, this piece echoes the album's title in that the narrator doubts if he has the courage to fly away. Thus, McTell establishes his own weaknesses, his side of the human window, and shows that, like the listener, he struggles to face some of life's challenges. Uncertainty and hesitation are eventually trumped by a decisive approach to problem-solving. The song is interesting both musically (especially John Marshall's sensitive drumming) and lyrically, featuring an appropriately gritty arrangement.

'Silver Birch And Weeping Willow' (McTell)
The kind of lovely, gentle composition at which McTell excels, this brief number echoes 'Kew Garden' in that it again portrays a tryst. This one is resolved differently, however, by the quiet but still dramatic insertion of a brief 'hello' (provided in the studio by an unknown office worker) that indicates the narrator's patience has been rewarded. The subtle contrasts of sexual highs and lows are reflected by the imagery of the stiff birch and the drooping willow. Mary Hopkin included the song on the same album that contained her interpretation of 'Kew Gardens'.

You Well Meaning Brought Me Here (1971)

Personnel:
Ralph McTell: guitar, vocals, piano, harmonica, harmonium, flute on 'Lay Your Money Down', Moog synthesizer on 'Genesis I Verse 20'
Rick Wakeman: organ, piano
Davey Johnstone: mandolin
Johnny Van Derek: violin
Caleb Quaye: electric guitar on 'Old Brown Dog'
Danny Thompson: double bass
Steve Bonnett: bass, piano
Roger Pope: drums
Mike Vickers: Moog synthesizer on 'Genesis I Verse 20'
Christine Holmes: backing vocals on 'Claudia'
Barry St. John: backing vocals on 'Claudia'
Judy Powell: backing vocals on 'Claudia'
Liza Strike: backing vocals on 'Claudia'
Gus Dudgeon: backing vocals on 'First And Last Man'
Sheila Dudgeon: backing vocals on 'First And Last Man'
Produced at Trident Studios by Gus Dudgeon
UK release date: 1971
US release date: 1971.
Highest chart places: did not chart
Running time: 42:57

McTell's first album for his new label (Famous) is one of his best and certainly his heaviest. If McTell was, in his own words, 'adrift on a sea of doubt' at the time of its recording, the inner turmoil produced a collection of great merit. While it is, of course, possible to create compelling art when one is happy, many artists have produced some of their best work while confused or unsettled. Dylan's *Blood On The Tracks* is one of many examples that could be cited. In his brief but insightful liner notes, Ian Pollock notes that despite McTell's unrest at the time, he still manages to connect with his audience. If McTell is 'travelling his own path', he is 'still sympathetically aware of yours and mine'. Many of the songs included in the collection are among the most interesting McTell has written to date and Gus Dudgeon's contributions as producer are more assured than his earlier work with the artist. Finally, McTell surrounds himself with an all-star cast of supporting musicians, including, among others, double bass maestro Danny Thompson, Rick Wakeman (of Yes fame) and Caleb Quaye, who contributed to sessions with the likes of Elton John, Mick Jagger and Paul McCartney. A perfect storm of talent, ambition, confusion and musicianship, the album succeeds on almost every level. If some artists are able to compose moving love songs or pieces of fascinating introspection, few have the capacity to effectively take on grander subjects, such as McTell does on this and subsequent albums. The cover photo depicts the lanky McTell, appropriately clad in earth tones, looking determined and serious. The word 'you' from the title is disproportionately large, perhaps hinting at the role McTell's listeners have played in his unease.

In his *Allmusic.com* review of the CD release, William Ruhlmann calls the album not only McTell's finest to date but one of the seminal singer-songwriter collections of the 1970s. He sees it as divided, if somewhat unevenly, between songs of gravitas and those that explore specific characters and their stories. He concludes by noting that 'the whole album reflects McTell's broad experience, especially of some of the seamier sides of life'.

'Genesis I Verse 20' (McTell)
In the King James version of the Bible, this passage runs as follows: 'And God said, "Let the waters bring forth abundantly the moving creature that hath life and fowl that may fly above the earth in the open firmament of heaven"'. McTell employs words like 'lo' and ''twixt' to lend the song an archaic feel and freely piles up biblical imagery to invoke an otherworldly mood to the piece. Hockenhull helpfully explains its penultimate line. During McTell's long spell in the hospital as a child, he delighted in a picture book that included a certain 'giant lizard of Tendagaroo', about which he used to dream. In *Angel Laughter* (83), McTell remembers the first time he was told about Genesis I, Verse 20, by the Rev. Bustin in Sunday School during a discussion about amoebae and water as the origin of life. Artists are creators in their own right, of course, and here, McTell wonders at the majesty of inception, just as listeners often marvel at the source of the music that so delights and fascinates us. All in all, it is a mystical track to commence McTell's most magical and visionary album.

'First And Last Man' (McTell)
Frederick Woods, editor of the *Oxford Book Of English Traditional Verse*, felt so strongly about this piece that he chose to include it in the 'Tradition in the Making' section of the anthology that includes folk songs like 'Barbara Allen' and 'The Foggy Dew'. Inspired by a picture based on American Cyrus Dallin's (1861-1944) 'Appeal to the Great Spirit' sculpture, 'First and Last Man' is a logical follow-up to the album's first track that ends with a reference to God's creation of man. As a concession to the primitive nature of the song's object, McTell intentionally creates a lyric that is imperfect. At such an early stage of life, of course, arts such as poetry have not fully matured. This is another song of creation. Images of seeds and procreation abound. Pain is associated with birth, but such suffering can be beautiful, just as the agony of the artistic process can yield handsome rewards. Indeed, the 'maker of music' is specifically mentioned and associated with magic. The monastic-sounding backing vocals strike an appropriate note and accentuate the song's rather ominous message.

'In Some Way I Loved You' (McTell)

McTell here returns the listener to the contemporary world with a playful variation on the one-night-stand song. This transition is unsettling after the grave nature of the first two tracks, but also a welcome relief, as such gravitas can be enervating. If the topic of the album's third song is rather common, McTell's approach is anything but commonplace. He shows his artistry by chronicling the affair not from the safety of the past but instead as it is unfolding. Though both parties willingly consent to the rendezvous, the narrator detects some hesitation on the part of his intended. His claim that, in some way, he really does love her comes off as both mischievous and genuine. On the other hand, it is easy to see how the composition might land its creator in hot water as well. The folk-rock accompaniment, nicely augmented by Johnny Van Derek's fiddle work, demonstrates that McTell can operate effectively with an ensemble and his casual 'la las' hint at the song's intended tone.

'Lay Your Money Down' (McTell)

This track features an interesting harmonium introduction played by McTell before the lyrics place us in the middle of the plot with the use of the word 'so'. Bars are often the setting for philosophical conversations, and here, the narrator, the pub's landlady and a war veteran attempt to make sense of some of life's mysteries. The simple insistence of the chorus implies that no matter how much we might philosophise, we must ultimately get down to business and take a stance. The war veteran's parting claim that 'time is money' underlines this approach, though the narrator seems far from convinced and doubts the older man's motives. The generation gap portrayed in the song has not been bridged. The full-throated vocal contributions to the chorus, augmented by McTell's contributions on flute, pick up on the piece's pub setting.

'Old Brown Dog' (McTell)

This moving song that extolls the dignity of age was inspired by a story and accompanying comic strip McTell saw in a boy's magazine (*Top Spot*) that had been reprinted from the *Saturday Evening Post*. In some ways, it anticipates one of his most famous compositions, 'Naomi', and also picks up the theme of how to properly say farewell treated earlier in 'Terminus' and later in 'The Setting'. Caleb Quaye's guitar solo, mixed through a Leslie cabinet, brilliantly captures the last moments of the dog's life force, still so strong, if now on its last legs.

'Pick Up A Gun' (McTell)

This song is a bitter attack against the British Army in particular and armies in general. McTell spent the worst six months of his life in the Queen's Surrey Regiment Junior Leader's Battalion at the age of 15, enduring humiliating hazing from his fellow cadets, mistreatment at the hands of officers, physical torment and verbal abuse. In some ways, this is his first mature protest song; he indicts a societal system that deceives and frightens young men. McTell assigns blame to the press, the politicians, writers who extoll the dubious glories of war and even the clergy who passively add their scant consolation to each soldier's burial. Little wonder, then, that so many young men are seduced into running away from home and into the army. The song ends powerfully with McTell, the former soldier, stating that, in his case, at least, the cycle will be broken: the armed forces won't get their hands on his son. This conclusion thus echoes the end of the famous folk song, 'Johnny, I Hardly Knew Ye', that states, 'they never will take our sons again'. Finally, it is interesting to recall that McTell followed his own father's footsteps by entering the service at a tender age.

'You Well Meaning Brought Me Here' (McTell)
Addressed to his audience, his management, but, even more importantly, to himself, this fascinating song is a lament that begins by asking where it all went wrong and ends with the mollifying lines that the narrator has, at the very least given his best effort. Given the fact that it was written when his career was on a definite upswing, some might view the song as a rather strange sentiment. What success he has achieved (such as appearing in front of huge crowds at the 1970 *Isle of Wight Festival*) has come as a surprise. Somehow McTell feels alienated and, just as Denslow had earlier mentioned in his liner notes to *My Side of Your Window*, 'on the outside'. Success has come at a price. The words of the critics hurt him; the pressures of the industry appalled and intimidated him. The song is an attempt to explain himself to his fans, but also, more importantly, to raise questions that, in the end, he must answer himself. These are the words of an artist full of talent but also full of self-doubt and suspicious of the real meaning of success. The piece avoids a feeling of self-pity due to the convincing and honest nature of its narrator. The rather formal-sounding piano introduction sets the stage for the song's serious nature and is later underscored by a light horn arrangement.

'Chalkdust' (McTell)
Desperately lonely characters populate the world of McTell's songs. Miss Johnson, the generically named central figure in 'Chalkdust', is a teacher of girls whose youth serves to remind her that she is rapidly ageing. They are her tormentors, both with the questions they ask in biology class and the manner in which they slander her, the old maid, via whispered gossip in the playground and nasty words written on the chalkboard. Her emotional vacuum and physical yearnings are filled only by chalk dust, conjuring images of our beginnings and our ultimate fate. Perhaps saddest of all is the fact that the chalk dust is derived from her very own creations, the 'hard planned lessons of another day'. Only the custodian has the gallantry or good manners

to wish her good night. Some elements of the song remain elusive. Perhaps Miss Johnson once had a suitor, whose name hangs 'in the hall/On a dusty roll of honour, unread on the wall'. Perhaps today it has all simply become too much, and the letters 'that she slips beneath the doors' are farewell letters announcing her resignation. At any rate, McTell's imagery in the song is compelling. As the piece ends, one feels her elegiac phrase must surely be altered to read 'Ashes to ashes, chalk dust to chalk dust'.

'The Ballad Of Dancing Doreen' (McTell)

Similar in some ways to the preceding track, 'The Ballad of Dancing Doreen' starts modestly enough, describing Doreen and her partner, Brian, as they compete in a ballroom dance. They do their best, eager to impress the judges, but another couple wins the competition. Brian cries, but the effect of the judges' decision is apparently more than Doreen can bear. McTell uses repeated parallel construction in the chorus to portray Doreen's breakdown. Now, lyrical details from early verses we may have ignored bear closer inspection. Has Doreen really spent her evenings sewing 2000 sequins by hand on her gown? She clearly suffers delusions of grandeur, innocent enough at first inspection but perhaps damning by the song's end. She is a queen and Brian is her king. Inspired in part by the BBC show, 'Come Dancing', McTell sees the song (16 February 2003 email to the author) as a sort of satire, but more importantly, a 'plea for sympathy and understanding as the humdrum lives, momentarily lifted by the waves of music and finery, are hurled against the rocks of reality'.

'Claudia' (McTell)

This song about racism was inspired by two separate events. McTell witnessed a man being beaten up because he was white, and while on tour in America, he met a woman in Harlem named Claudia, who was involved with the Black Panther movement. A powerful woman, she impressed the young McTell with her conviction. McTell (interview with author, 20 December 2022): 'It was a chance for me to address the incident with someone who had a more clear-cut view of the situation'. He wrote the piece (Hockenhull, 64) 'to make a point that it's no good just talking about equality – you've got to get up and do something about it'. In other words, eventually, you have to lay your money down. The lyrics are complemented by a jaunty, upbeat tune, replete with clever piano and guitar fills. McTell's strong lead vocal gains further power from the contributions made by backing singers Christine Holmes, Barry St. John, Judy Powell and Liza Strike. Overall, one of the songwriter's most effective folk-rock pieces.

'The Ferryman' (McTell)

McTell's longest composition, and certainly one of his best, 'The Ferryman' warrants a rather lengthy explication. In 1940, Woody Guthrie was asked to write a song about John Huston's motion picture adaptation of Steinbeck's epic novel, *The Grapes Of Wrath*. Guthrie agreed and, fuelled both by his compassion for the plight of the Okies and a half-gallon jug of wine, distilled the story into a 17-verse piece he called 'Tom Joad'. 31 years later, Ralph McTell pulled off a similar feat, choosing Hermann Hesse's novella, Siddhartha, as the basis for his song, 'The Ferryman'. McTell's piece succeeds both as a summary of Hesse's work and a metaphorical statement of his own development as an artist.

Briefly, the famous Bildungsroman tells the story of Siddhartha, the gifted son of a Brahmin, who grows disenchanted with his life and sets out on the road to self-discovery. Along the way, the seeker first meets a band of ascetics and then Gotama, the historical Buddha himself. After a period in which he falls under the spell of earthly pleasures in the form of a profitable business and a famous courtesan, Siddhartha resumes his quest to achieve Nirvana. His wanderings take him to a river, where he meets Vasudeva, an elderly ferryman. Both from the ferryman and the river itself, Siddhartha learns the unity of all things and achieves Nirvana, a state of peace in which the self is absorbed into what Norbert Wiener calls 'the Great Soul of the World'.

Aged 27 when he wrote 'The Ferryman', McTell was already an experienced traveller, having spent years pursuing Woody Guthrie's vagabond existence. Though he is reaching the height of his artistic power, McTell still seems unsure of a great many things and is suffering a bit of a crisis. 'The Ferryman' helps to shed some light on this apparent paradox. McTell's role as creator is underscored by his use of 'behold, I give you, I give you the travelling man' at its very beginning. Similarly, the third line includes the use of 'lo, and I give you the travelling man'. Words like 'lo' and 'behold' suggest that McTell, the creator, can be seen as a magician of sorts. Such usage also nicely picks up the tone of Hesse's mystical work, as do the string arrangements of Robert Kirby and the harp flourishes heard midway through the track and at its conclusion.

That we can associate McTell with the traveller in his song is reflected by his depiction of one who is 'very heavy laden with the questions in his burden'. As mentioned above, such burdens are neatly outlined in 'You Well Meaning Brought Me Here'. McTell and the traveller have quite literally 'crossed the mountains', 'forded streams' and 'spent a long time surviving on his dreams'. The demands of the physical world – a body of water is here identified for the first time as an obstacle that must be crossed – are thus identified, but so is the lure of the dream world of the artist's imagination. As they progress through life, McTell/the traveller/Siddhartha all experience the disparate, if equally alluring, worlds of material and imaginative pleasure.

The first verse ends with the couplet: 'Many times he's tried to lighten up his heavy load/But his compromises fail him and he ends back on the road'. Often, the artist turns to drink and/or drugs to lighten his burdens, or he may sacrifice his artistic vision in order to become more popular or make more money. McTell rightly identifies the ultimate failure of both these approaches. He has doubtless felt their temptations himself, only to end up 'back on the road' in his search for artistic fulfilment. Here, as in the novella, 'the road' is identified as a positive option. It implies that the seeker is still seeking; he has not settled on one answer.

Still, such quests are demanding and exhausting; self-knowledge, Nirvana, artistic fulfilment – call it what you will – are gained only by enervating effort. The road can seem 'never-ending'. Surely, the artist wonders, someone else has travelled the same road and can act as a guide or 'saviour' for the pilgrim. While his finished product can temporarily satisfy him, a true artist never grows complacent. These demands may lead the artist to yearn for an additional release or source of fulfilment. Religious faith is one such alternative to art. McTell himself has felt the attraction of faith and displays it in songs such as the aptly titled, 'Sometimes I Wish I Could Pray' (discussed later).

While Siddhartha encounters first the sect of the Samanas and later the Buddha himself, he decides that neither provides exactly what he is seeking. In the same way, we may read the lines, 'he has cried aloud for a saviour/And in vain for a teacher, someone to lighten up the load', as McTell's realisation that much as he might revere his earliest heroes – Guthrie, Wizz Jones, Arthur Blake, Blind Willie McTell, Reverend Gary Davis to mention just a few – he must create and stand by his own work rather than simply imitate the approaches taken by them. The very next line, in fact, shows him tipping his hat to Bob Dylan's 1962 composition, 'A Hard Rain's A-Gonna Fall': 'And he's heard the sounds of war in a gentle shower of rain'. Like any artist, McTell has heard 'the whisperings of despair that he could not explain'. Often, the artist must wonder why he is putting himself through such torment. Where is the reward in an art that demands that one is never satisfied with one's creations? Put another way, why, McTell wonders, does he still feel so empty and full of doubt even after creating a masterpiece like *You Well Meaning Brought Me Here*? Must there always be a 'reason for his journey'? Can art in itself not be enough?

The third verse provides a possible solution: a river beautiful and wide but with treacherous currents. McTell's predilection for water imagery is demonstrated in songs such as 'Barges', 'Bridge Of Sighs', 'River Rising' and 'Throw Out A Line And Dream'. Here, the river is a border, a division that stands between the seeker and his goal. If he has, at least temporarily, seen the need to journey on alone for ultimate satisfaction, McTell/the traveller/Siddhartha now realises he will need help in overcoming this obstacle. While McTell must create his own art to reach artistic nirvana, he realises it would be impossible without the guidance and inspiration of his musical heroes, dead and alive. Who, then, is the ferryman 'strong enough to row against the tide'?

The ferryman is someone older, wiser and more experienced. For significantly different reasons, Siddhartha and McTell are both fatherless. They have come a long way on their own, but now need the kind of assistance often supplied by a paternal figure. (Interestingly enough, Siddhartha's own son later rejects him just as Siddhartha did his own father. McTell does not touch on this in his song). The river itself plays an active role in the journey: 'And the ferryman was old, but he moved the boat so well/Or did the river move the boat?/The traveller could not tell'. The river is, in fact, a major character in Hesse's novella. In his first encounter with Siddhartha, the Ferryman tells him that one thing he has learned from the river is that 'everything comes again'. Thus, the concept of Karma is introduced. In a later encounter with the river, Siddhartha indicates his desire to learn from the river: 'The man who grasped this water and its secrets, so it seemed, would also grasp a lot of other things, many secrets, all secrets'. The river is both a challenge to the artist and, more importantly, a possible muse. The river is a divide between the artistic and the non-artistic world, between satisfaction and frustration. In the song, the traveller closes his eyes and listens to the 'murmuring' of the river 'and the beating of his heart'. In a sense, the two are now one. The river and all it stands for is the traveller's lifeblood.

Now, finally, the traveller is rewarded. He hears the river laughing and he hears the river crying. In the river, he hears 'the beauty and the sadness of the world'. He hears both the sound of dying and the sound of birth. Equipped now with the necessary patience and humility, the aspirant has become an artist. He has listened to what the river and the Ferryman have been trying to teach him. He realises the dichotomies of life and how necessary to artistic achievement is the understanding of both. 'The sounds blended together and they became a whole/And the rhythm was his heartbeat to the music in his soul'. The traveller has crossed the river; the artist has realised his vision and has become one with his art. Just as the soul outlives the body, so will the artist's creations outlive him.

The song's last verse beautifully illustrates one of Buddhism's teachings: that all life is connected. Just as Siddhartha eventually becomes a Ferryman himself, so the traveller in McTell's song becomes the river, boat and Ferryman, and, further, 'the journey and the song that the singing river sang'. His learning phase complete, the artist opens his eyes to a world both real and merged with his imagination. The Ferryman has played his part in the development of the artist. The artist has become the Ferryman himself. As McTell pulls us back from an individual's story to the world at large, we see the artist's role more clearly. Just as the artist/traveller has learned the necessity of humility, McTell displays such humility by merging the individual with the natural forces of the world. The artistic process has come full circle.

Not Till Tomorrow (1972)

Personnel:
Ralph McTell: guitar, vocals, piano, organ, harmonica
Tony Visconti: sitar, Hammond organ, recorder, backing vocals
Mary Hopkin: backing vocals (listed as Mary Visconti)
Danny Thompson: double bass
Laurie Allan: percussion
Produced at Air Studios and Sound Techniques Studio by Tony Visconti in 1972
UK release date: November 1972
US release date: 1973
Highest chart places: UK: 36
Running time: 45:51

More modest in scope and ambition than its predecessor, *Not Till Tomorrow* is nonetheless nearly as strong. Songs of childhood and childhood heroes are paired with those of love, both enduring and fleeting. Perhaps the most powerful tracks, however, are the ones that continue to explore the artist's dilemma, 'Zimmerman Blues' and 'Sylvia'. Tony Visconti's light-touch production is consistently appropriate to these grounded compositions. McTell felt more comfortable working with Visconti than he had earlier with Dudgeon. While some may search for hidden meaning in the album's title, the truth is more every day. When asked by the printer when the title might be chosen, manager Jo Lustig's secretary replied, 'Oh, not till tomorrow'. The cover photo depicts a nonchalant, cool McTell, cigarette (no doubt a Gauloises) dangling from his mouth, and again reflects the artist's fear of being regarded as a softie.

William Ruhlmann's review for *Allmusic.com* focuses on what might have been. He believes that Warner Bros. had hoped McTell might become another Cat Stevens or James Taylor. Instead, the company found themselves dealing with an artist 'uncomfortable with his growing renown, unlikely to spend much time in the States and more interested in local concerns'. Ruhlmann's conclusion that songs like 'Barges' and 'Nettle Wine' are too English and personal to attract the larger listening audience the label had hoped for is largely accurate. Indeed, McTell himself recognises that (Awde, 178) 'essentially, I'm English and what I do is English, and my past is there. I couldn't really have adapted and been totally happy with it. I have to do what I do'.

'Zimmerman Blues' (McTell)

The opening track is dedicated to, or at least inspired by, the artistic and personal predicaments facing Bob Dylan (né Zimmerman) in the early 1970s. In a sense, the song reflects a thickening of McTell's skin. He is speaking not just for himself but for all artists who have been used by the system to create revenue at the cost of their integrity or vision. The song is a dialogue of sorts between the artist and the consumer of his art. So what, in the end, do the 'Zimmerman Blues' entail? Perhaps the best answer is the alienated relationship between the artist and his audience. With his innocent days of inspiration behind him, the artist is now unsure how to proceed except to follow his conscience and his aesthetic instincts.

'First Song' (McTell)
Though markedly different in tone from the preceding track, 'First Song' is also the work of an artist in that it acknowledges both the power of words and their impotence. It is also a song of separation, self-knowledge and the inevitability of change. McTell repeats an open-ended chorus at the conclusion of each verse to heighten the tension. He has perhaps picked up this technique from his country blues mentors (see 'Hesitation Blues'). The narrator expresses hope for the future and reassures his love that amid all the changes in his life, she will remain a constant. In the second verse, he admits that the temptation to revert to old habits still exists. The pattern of self-doubt continues in the final verse, which opens with another question that is, however, swiftly answered. After these qualified explanations, the narrator is finally able to complete the chorus, resolve the tension and state that she is indeed his first song and that he loves her. Love rarely travels a level road; people and circumstances change. The perseverance of love, however, is equal to any challenge. The inclusion of a soft horn in the track is typical of Visconti's deft touch. All in all, a truly wonderful piece.

'When I Was A Cowboy' (McTell)
The album's second track is much more carefree and straightforward than its predecessor. Here, a father figure in the form of a sheriff lends his young disciple some practical advice. Like many young English boys, McTell was fascinated with the American West and cowboy heroes like Hopalong Cassidy. After listing the numerous dangers inherent in a cowboy's life, McTell serves up a punchline of sorts at the song's conclusion: that his actual life is less daunting than this imagined existence. McTell also acknowledges the influence of Lead Belly's 'Out on the Western Plains', whose opening line is identical to the title of McTell's piece. The song's rhythm is intentionally quirky and serves to heighten the contrasts inherent in the lyrics. The thorough understanding McTell and bassist Danny Thompson enjoy is on full display in the piece.

'Nettle Wine' (McTell)
Written while McTell was on a brief vacation in Wales, this bucolic piece features some intricate guitar work and is a regular part of his concert repertoire. Though the main theme is the creation of the titular beverage, McTell also muses on the creator of the house that he rents. In short, it is a homage to the creative process and thus qualifies as another of McTell's artist songs.

'Sylvia' (McTell)

Yet another 'artist' song, 'Sylvia' reveals McTell's empathy for Sylvia Plath, the American poet who died by her own hand. Plath is supposed to have awoken from an operation following a miscarriage to see tulips in her hospital room. In her poem, 'Tulips', referenced here by McTell, the poet writes that, 'Nobody watched me before, now I am watched'. Surely, this line spoke to McTell, the singer who has been exposed to public scrutiny, even by those who meant well. While expressing a sincere admiration for the dead poet, McTell is also reassuring or reminding himself on one of his own days of self-doubt that his songs help those thousands in the record-buying public whom he will never know. Listening to the song, we are privy to what must sadly remain a one-sided conversation between two artists who have suffered in different ways. Though he is not an accomplished pianist, McTell's accompaniment here is handled well.

'Birdman' (McTell)

Dedicated to American activist George Jackson (1941-71), 'Birdman' extolls the virtues of freedom and was based loosely on the legend of John Henry. McTell (20 May 2003 interview with the author): 'George's lessons of life touched me very deeply. I felt that George was so articulate, that he was so rational, that no system would dare kill this man. No system would dare close his mouth'. Jackson was, in fact, killed under mysterious circumstances, 'shot while trying to escape'. 'You can't beat the system if the system wants you out', McTell concludes dolefully before adding that Jackson's death signalled the end of his youthful idealism. McTell's guitar here recalls some of his best blues work, while his reverb-drenched vocals are spirited.

'Barges' (McTell)

One of his most evocative songs, 'Barges' draws heavily on McTell's childhood. McTell is masterful at setting an atmosphere for his songs with their musical accompaniment. In this case, in addition to McTell's always-sublime fingerpicked guitar (that serves to mimic the rippling water), Tony Visconti's recorder completely captures the listener's attention before the first word is sung. The composition, both sentimental and wistful, describes an outing (or, more probably, an amalgam of such outings) taken by McTell and his brother while on summer holiday at their aunt Olive's in Banbury. They are city boys in a country boy's world, shy and happy, but also ever mindful of their distant mother. Their worries for her are emotional baggage they take with them, even on a jaunt like this. Similarly, the weight of their fatherless childhood is apparent in the second line of the third verse. In this case, the 'man' is the bargeman, but one feels he is a sort of surrogate father, if only for the briefest moment. In some ways, this recalls McTell's interest in Hesse's Ferryman discussed earlier. The song concludes with the syntactically challenging and possibly ambiguous line that again references the man. In this case, he is most probably the mature McTell looking back fondly on his childhood, but it could also be the bargeman mentioned earlier, so happy in his work. Throughout the piece, McTell stresses the importance of allowing yourself to release your memories to explore them in order to progress and mature in life.

'Standing Down In New York Town' (McTell)
Undoubtedly inspired by Woody Guthrie's song, 'New York Town', which begins with the line from which this McTell composition takes its title, this piece explores homesickness and privilege. While on tour, McTell had just left his posh hotel when he was approached by a man seeking assistance so that he could get back home. Hopalong Cassidy is referenced here and serves to contrast the romantic notions of America, that young McTell once held with the angry slogans (including 'Avenge Attica!') and screaming sirens he now encounters. McTell's vocals are especially plaintive, reflecting the ache and helplessness he feels.

'Another Rain Has Fallen' (McTell)
A very gentle track that features only McTell and his guitar, this song is a rumination on the alternately positive and negative nature of precipitation and is in some ways similar to Paul McCartney's contemporaneous, 'Mamunia'. One can also characterise the lyric as a variation on Galatians 6:7, typically translated as, 'whatever a man sows, that shall he also reap'. Throughout the performance, McTell's voice and guitar onomatopoeically mimic the sound of falling rain.

'This Time Of Night' (McTell)
A rather cryptic song, 'This Time Of Night' depicts the narrator's desire to end a conversation, an encounter, after things have run their course and reached a climax. Sexual temptation is a theme that recurs in many of McTell's songs. In an interview with the author (20 May 2003), McTell remarks: 'The whole thing about holding things together at home and holding relationships together is hard and you can't always write directly about it, one has to allude to these things. There's this tremendous power of sexuality, it's all around you, and it's coming at you from wherever you look, so you resort to poems'. He adds, 'I always remember George Melly, who was so glad when his libido finally dropped because it was like being unchained. It's like anywhere you go, you've got this lunatic on a chain'. At this time of night, such chains are still all too apparent. Later in his recording career, McTell will celebrate the powers of a woman's forgiveness in 'Seeds Of Heaven'. In this case, however, the narrator anticipates no such absolution and sees no future for what is most likely an illicit relationship whose unhappy conclusion was inevitable. McTell strums rather than fingerpicks here, adding punch to the track that is accentuated by Danny Thompson's bass and Laurie Allan's drumming.

'Gypsy' (McTell)

Here, McTell, the outsider, expresses empathy for travellers (when the song was composed, the term, 'gypsy', did not carry the negative connotations it does today) who live outside the mainstream of life. Indeed, McTell has expressed his belief that he may have Romani blood in him. The song's message is one of both compassion on McTell's part and defiance on the part of the Romani. Despite the fact that the world has tried to pen them in, the Romani remain proud of their restless traditions and their freedom, so coveted by gadjo boys (those of non-Romani blood). Ewan MacColl's 'Freeborn Man Of The Travelling People' explores similar themes, though in a somewhat gentler way. McTell bravely stretches his vocal range at times in this ambitious piece.

Easy (1974)

Personnel:
Ralph McTell: guitar, vocals, banjo, harmonium, harmonica
Wizz Jones: guitar
Bert Jansch: guitar on 'Run Johnny Run'
Danny Thompson: double bass, bass drum on 'Stuff No More'
Steve Bonnett: mandolin
Mike Piggott, Lynsey Scott: violin
Dave Mattacks: drums
Gerry Conway: drums
Michael Bennett: backing vocals
John Kongos: backing vocals on 'Run Johnny Run'
Davey Johnson: mandolin
Mick Bartlett: jug
Recorded at John Kongos Studio, Marquee Studio in 1974.
Produced by Ralph McTell, Danny Thompson and Tony Visconti.
UK release date: March 1974. US release date: 1978
Highest chart places: UK: 31
Running time: 31:04

Such are the vagaries of the music industry that this short album sold better than McTell's previous two efforts, both of which are, to this listener, far superior. *Easy* was awarded a silver disc in 1976 and charted at number 31. One senses that after the heaviness and soul-searching so apparent on *You Well Meaning* and *Not Till Tomorrow*, McTell was ready to have a bit of fun. Nonetheless, some fine tracks are included, such as 'Maginot Waltz', 'Zig Zag Line' and 'Summer Lightning'. This is McTell's shortest album and the closest he ever came to a pop sound and pop sensibility. 'Evening In The Pontine Marshes', a lovely painting by the Catalan artist Enrique Serra Auqué (1858-1918), adorns the cover.

Chris Nickson reviewed the CD release for *Allmusic.com* and praised McTell's picking ability, noting that McTell has included some of his most accessible material, specifically, 'Sweet Mystery' and 'Let Me Down Easy'. He sees 'Run Johnny Run' as a sign that McTell hasn't completely forsaken his roots in this attempt to find a wider audience. Rob Beattie reviewed the CD for *Q Magazine* in March 2000. He also admires 'Run Johnny Run' and 'Maginot Waltz' while describing 'Summer Lightning' and 'Let Me Down Easy' as among McTell's finest compositions. He tempers an otherwise positive review by deeming the collection 'stylistically predictable'.

'Take It Easy' (McTell)

The album's opening track pokes fun at the sort of braggadocio so often found in the blues tradition. A slight, short, up-tempo number, it features a catchy chorus and a nice fiddle solo.

'Maddy Dances' (McTell)
A homage to Maddy Prior, lead singer of Steeleye Span, this feel-good song features some first-rate drumming from Dave Mattacks. By way of returning the favour, Prior would appear on McTell's 1975 *Streets* album. Just as he has in numbers like 'Sylvia', McTell is happy to praise another artist, one whose art spreads joy.

'Maginot Waltz' (McTell)
A thoughtful, well-executed recording, 'Maginot Waltz' came to the composer out of nowhere and was completed in 40 minutes. The song's title is misleading in that the Maginot line was constructed between 1929-1938 and, thus, did not exist in 1914 when this song is set. McTell intentionally named one of the characters Albert, after his grandfather, Albert Henry Moss, who served in The Great War. The tune recalls 'England 1914' in its ominous foreshadowing, and the variation McTell plays on its opening G chord hints that the song isn't going where one thinks it might. McTell springs a surprise on listeners by waiting until the final verse to reveal that the narrator is soon to leave to fight in France. Numerous rests, tempo changes and McTell's harmonium lend the piece musical interest.

'Sweet Mystery' (McTell)
Since this track playfully contrasts romance and lust, McTell's almost sheepish vocals perfectly suit its tone. A chance remark from friend, Danny Thompson, occasioned the piece, which is somewhat similar to 'In Some Way I Loved You', this time downplaying the role of sex and praising the more subtle approach that retains the sense of mystery so vital to the early days of courtship. The repeated use of the phrase, 'one of these days', that opens each verse slyly implies that the narrator will never realise his dream of emulating Fred Astaire. The old-fashioned-sounding violin contributes to the track's feel. Good fun.

'Stuff No More' (McTell)
An enjoyable, if slight, number that was largely improvised in the studio and features the jug band sound McTell had, by then, largely abandoned. Mick 'Henry the VIII' Bartlett plays jug on the track and McTell has since fondly recalled in *Summer Lightning* how important and inspirational his enthusiasm and high spirits were to his early days as a performer.

'Run Johnny Run' (McTell)
The crooked nature of this song suits the flight of an escaping prisoner. McTell has stated that he abandoned his usual rhyme scheme approach to provide the track with a certain jagged quality. Images of transcendence and freedom pervade the piece, while sky imagery dominates its final verse. McTell may have been inspired by the traditional American folk song, 'Lost

John', which also features a man on the run. McTell greatly admired the guitar stylings of Bert Jansch, who guests on this track, calling him (Bean, 219) 'the most important thing that happened to the British acoustic guitar scene, much more important than many of the others that have got bigger reputations'.

'Zig Zag Line' (McTell)
'Zig Zag Line' is based on a climb McTell took with his son, Sam. Ascending a hill is a wonderfully simple metaphor for the challenges of parenting. In this case, the climb is steep enough that the father and son must traverse the slope slowly, gradually, in a zigzag fashion. Often a direct route is impossible. Yet, both seem quite happy to make the effort. The silent language of looks, shared grins and held hands speaks eloquently to the real bond that is apparent. Deprived of his own father's company, McTell delights in the simple fact that he is together with his son and that 'he knew me and you know I knew him'. Many fathers might take such togetherness for granted, but McTell realises how lucky he is and isn't ashamed to celebrate the fact in song. The composer has also stated that he was thinking of the biblical story of Abraham and Isaac when he conceived the piece.

'Let Me Down Easy' (McTell)
In three spare verses set to a waltz time, 'Let Me Down Easy' details a breakup from the perspective of a lover who knows the end is near. The augmented opening chord immediately sets the tone for this moving piece. The earnest plea of the chorus is one familiar to most listeners, yet McTell's aching vocal delivery distinguishes the song. Instead of waiting to hear the bad news from his lover, the narrator is making a preemptive appeal for mercy. In contrast to the vagueness of the first verse, the second employs a sailing metaphor that may provide consolation to the narrator. The relationship seems somehow doomed by nature itself. The third verse mirrors the first in structure, and while it finds the narrator still struggling to express himself, his lover's compassion lends him some solace. In direct contrast to the inexperienced lovers in songs like 'Grande Affaire' and 'Summer Girls', the narrator of 'Let Me Down Easy' speaks from a more mature perspective. Various tempo changes and modulations aptly mirror the uncertainties portrayed in the piece.

'Would I Lie To You' (McTell)
A very simple number that really swings, 'Would I Lie to You' is distinguished by Danny Thompson's wonderful double bass introduction. Perhaps it is songs like this, featuring stock rhymes such as die/sigh/cry and you/true, that made the album so popular with listeners.

'Summer Lightning' (McTell)
The album's last track is also its finest. Summer lightning (also known as heat lighting or silent lightning) is visible, but distant and ultimately benign, and

thus serves as a well-chosen metaphor for the type of argument not unusual in marriage. How many of us have used reconciliatory phrases similar to those McTell employs here? McTell's vocals perfectly suit the tone of the piece and demonstrate the compassionate expressiveness so characteristic of his work. He stated that in the song, he wished to capture the pregnant moments of silence that sometimes occur between even the most intimate of couples.

Tracks Included on the CD Release:
'Teacher Teacher' (McTell)
Recorded with the T. Rex rhythm section, this selection features a catchy chorus and highlights the differences between academic learning and the lessons that result from more actively engaging in (real) life. Released as a single in 1972.

'Truckin' Lil Baby' (McTell)
Recorded with the same personnel as 'Teacher Teacher', this silly but infectious track relies on well-known blues conventions and seems to have been written for fun rather than posterity. It also appears on McTell's 1988 album of blues covers, *Blue Skies Black Heroes*.

Streets (1975)

Personnel:
Ralph McTell: guitar, piano, harmonica, vocals
Rod Clements: bass
Dave Pegg: bass
Danny Lane: drums, percussion
Bob Kerr: saxophone
Danny Thompson: double bass
Peter Berryman: guitar
Prelude: backing vocals
Kokomo: backing vocals on 'Another Star Ascending'
Rabbit Bundrick: piano, Hammond organ
Jerry Donahue: guitar
Mike Piggott: guitar, violin
Sammy Mitchel: national guitar
Clem Cattani: drums
Hank Devito: steel guitar
Jim Parker: piano
Sandy Spencer: cello on 'Red Apple Juice'
Alan Harris: jaw harp 'Red Apple Juice'
Andy Cronshaw: zither
Ron Edwards: piano
Maddy Prior: backing vocals on 'Lunar Lullaby'
Recorded at Nova Sound Recording Studios.
Produced by Ralph McTell
Release date: 1975
Highest chart places: UK: 13
Running time: 39:54

McTell's first post-hit album for Warner Bros. earned him a career-best spot of number 13 on the charts. Like *Easy* before it, however, it is far from his strongest collection of songs. Most are minor, another is a cover and two can be considered throwaways. To this listener, only a few stand out: 'Grande Affaire', 'Heron Song' and 'Lunar Lullaby'. This is a pity since McTell's production is largely tasteful and the musicians used to record the album are first class. McTell had not been entirely happy with the drummers on his previous collections, feeling they were not attuned to the sound he was after. For *Streets*, he employed American Danny Lane in this role and was very pleased with his sensitive percussion work. A photograph of McTell, looking somewhat surprised to be caught in the act of lighting up a cigarette, serves as cover art. This image was a homage of sorts to a photograph of Georgia Tom (Thomas A. Dorsey, 1899-1993), a performer of blues and gospel music.

Reviewing the CD release of the album for *Allmusic.com*, Chris Nickson deems the tracks good but not essential. 'Grande Affaire' is described as 'pleasant', while 'Heron Song' is 'almost vintage '60s McTell in its straightforwardness. The ragtime influence of much of his early playing has gone and what remains is someone who's found himself. If you're looking for a best of, however, look on'. The latter comment stems from the assumption some might have made from the album's title and its inclusion of McTell's big hit.

'Streets Of London' (McTell)
After the song became a huge hit, McTell and his manager, brother Bruce May, both fought hard to omit this track from the album, arguing against overexposure and fearing that he would be accused of ripping off the record-buying public. Obviously, his efforts were in vain. A small victory they won was in having the album titled simply *Streets* instead of Warner Bros.' desire to name it after the hit single.

'You Make Me Feel Good' (McTell)
Here, McTell celebrates his relationship with his daughter, Leah. As background to the description of his down-to-earth offspring, McTell uses a series of opposites, noting his preference for dandelions over gardenias, sparrows to birds of paradise and things one can rely on as opposed to 'things you can't control'. The fact that he can rely on her to be herself is enough to make her father feel good. Like most tracks on the album, the accompaniment has a gentle pop-rock feel. The vocal harmony group Prelude provide backing vocals and Bob Kerr adds saxophone.

'Grande Affaire' (McTell)
This composition had a long genesis, having first been written in 1971. Just as he has on some earlier selections, McTell here pokes fun at the conventions of love. In the first half of the song, its penny-pinching narrator catalogues a long list of ways in which he is not the conventional lover: he takes the bus instead of a car, shares his lover's meal instead of ordering his own and stays at a 'room without any view'. He is able to joke about these early days from the perspective of a man who is now, by comparison, financially comfortable. The charm of the song lies in the fact that the self-deprecating narrator is not entirely at home in his new world, one where white-coated waiters attend him and various posh temptations lie in wait. Though the piece is lighthearted in nature, the line, 'frightened of meeting someone that we knew', has more sinister associations. When they started to see each other, Nanna was still involved with an American named Bill. Things remained unresolved in the love triangle until, one evening, a violent altercation ended Bill's relationship with Nanna. McTell has admitted that the pidgin French title he concocted for the piece actually means something akin to 'big business transaction'. The song remains a favourite of both the composer and this listener.

'El Progresso' (McTell)
A playful track with both a flamenco and mariachi feel, 'El Progresso' is most notable for its unusual time signature. It is perhaps best regarded as a joke that fails to come off.

'Red Apple Juice' (trad.)
A strong piece that is an amalgam of a few old country blues numbers (including 'Honey Babe Blues', 'Sugar Babe' or 'Sugar Baby') and was recorded with a live vocal in a single take. Sandy Spencer's cello is an interesting addition to a blues track.

'Heron Song' (McTell)
This powerful composition reflects the anguish that separation can bring and stems from one of the lowest moments of McTell's life. On the road in Europe, he was broke, his guitar had recently been shattered, he was starving and he feared he was losing the love of his life. In short, he felt utterly bereft. The song's first and third verses begin with the conjunction, 'and', as if to suggest that the hurt is still present. So haunted is the wandering narrator by the memories of his lover that he employs the verb, 'to carry', to reflect the burden her memory has become. The road is his other constant companion, implying perhaps that his journey has been made as an attempt to flee the harsh truth of his situation: that the love affair seems doomed to failure. The song's dominant image, the heron, has wings and thus the ability to fly to his love. The narrator, on the other hand, must continue his journey, already 'a million miles' long, on foot. In stark contrast to him, rooted on the road, the regal bird is a transcendent figure. The dead tree that is his throne wonderfully evokes the bleakness of the narrator's predicament and serves as a mesmerising contrast to the bird itself. The final verse employs a subjunctive desire found often in folk songs, that of having wings with which to fly to the arms of the beloved. Gentle guitar fills and a delicate string arrangement lend atmosphere to the track.

'Pity The Boy' (McTell)
A gentle, acoustic song that is a variation of the age-old theme of choosing money and the security it brings over true love. The final verse introduces a child born from the union of two like-minded souls.

'Interest On The Loan' (McTell)
This track features Hank Devito's steel guitar and has a country-western feel. Its theme is the difficulty of communication and McTell employs a financial metaphor to make his point.

'Jenny Taylor/Je N'etais La' (McTell)
The fact that McTell can't finish his performance of this song without succumbing to laughter speaks volumes of its relative importance. The

French lyrics can be summarised as meaning, 'don't do it, it doesn't work like that'.

'Lunar Lullaby' (McTell)
This gentle song, originally intended for the *Easy* album, was inspired by an evening walk McTell took by the Thames. It employs sky and water imagery and examines the random and transitory nature of life. The uncertainty that pervades most of the piece is resolved at its conclusion. The composition features one of McTell's loveliest melodies and is not overwhelmed by the tasteful production touches used to augment it. McTell would later use a line from the song, 'Oh happy to watch the sun go down/And join the angel laughter', as the title for the first volume of his autobiography.

Tracks Recorded Included on the CD Release of Streets:
'Seeds Of Heaven' (McTell)
A strong composition that describes a woman's forgiveness as heaven-sent. This listener would have preferred it to have a place on the original album at the expense of some of its lightweight pieces. The track exemplifies the feel that drummer Danny Lane brings to the band.

'Another Star Ascending (The Boxer)' (McTell)
McTell is an avid fan of boxing, noting in his autobiography that his father was a regimental champion in his weight class and that the purchase of the *Freddie Mills Boxing Annual* was a highlight of McTell's childhood. Here, he finds some similarities between the courage needed to be a performer and the bravery required for those who lace on the gloves. McTell displays nothing but admiration for the pugilists and only scorn for those who merely regard them as entertainers or, even worse, any who profit from the fighters' valiant efforts. A much stronger track than many on the LP, it includes a good performance from the entire band and features a chorus that is both catchy and powerful.

Right Side Up (1976)

Personnel:
Ralph McTell: guitar, piano, vibraphone, vocals
Peter Swettenham: keyboards, backing vocals
Danny Thompson: double bass
John Stevens: drums
Pick Withers: drums
Rod Clements: bass
Dave Pegg: bass
Tony Rivers: backing vocals
Ken Gold: backing vocals
John Perry: backing vocals
Sam Mitchell: bottleneck guitar on 'Country Boys'
John Martyn: guitar on 'River Rising Moon High'
Dave Mitchell: saxophone
Graham Preskett: keyboards, violin
Jerry Donahue: guitar
Recorded at Air Studios, 1976.
Produced by Ralph McTell and Peter Swettenham.
Release date: 1976.
Highest chart places: did not chart.
Running time: 35:54

Right Side Up is an excellent album that includes some of McTell's best work, as well as two fine cover versions. 'Naomi', 'Tequila Sunset', 'Weather The Storm' and 'From Clare To Here' are all McTell classics that have stood the test of time. While the cover of the CD includes a rather bland photo of McTell, the impression left by the illustration on the LP is more striking. Here, we see a coin being tossed, about to land 'right side up'. This image is an accurate reflection of McTell's return to form following the sub-par *Streets* project. A possible theme that unites the work is the necessity of confronting difficult emotions. We age, grow lonely, experience homesickness and struggle to express our true feelings, but if we find the courage to recognise these challenges, we can weather such storms. Aided by Peter Swettenham, McTell's production is spot on throughout, managing to be impactful without drawing unnecessary attention to itself. The entire album sounds clean and smooth and shows that folk-pop can effectively treat subjects more important than broken hearts. It is one of the best-sung albums in McTell's catalogue.

Brett Hartenback reviewed the collection for *Allmusic.com*. While treading familiar ground with his observation that 'there's a timeless, almost traditional bent to McTell's writing', he notes how McTell's gift for melody 'is well suited to the record's quiet tales of love, friendship and the working class', and praises the understated nature of the album's production.

'San Diego Serenade' (Waits)
McTell has related a story in which he describes once playing craps with Waits, who had no idea who McTell was. At any rate, his high regard for the songwriter is such that he leads off his eighth album with a cover of one of the American's best compositions, a lovely song of remorse and regret that features numerous parallel constructions in its lyrics. McTell is far from alone in his regard for the piece. Nanci Griffith, Juice Newton, Cilla Black and Eric Andersen have all recorded their interpretations.

'Naomi' (McTell)
One of McTell's strongest and most beloved compositions, 'Naomi' celebrates perseverance and mature love. The narrator admits that 'age is for complaining', but the song is far from a lament. Instead, it details how the years have made him appreciate his companion. He admits to cheating on her in the past and acknowledges in the chorus that 'she wasn't all I wanted', but he tempers this observation with the wisdom that 'she's all I'll ever need'. The song closes with a touching compliment to Naomi: though she is not conventionally beautiful, Naomi makes the narrator 'feel like a man'. Besides the obvious sexual reference, the statement demonstrates how thoroughly Naomi has taught the narrator the most important lessons of life. McTell's vocals are touching without sounding lachrymose. The song's genesis centred around the fact that McTell had a great aunt named Naomi and had recently visited some elderly relatives. Interestingly, McTell wrote the last verse first. Though the song's sentiments seem personal upon first listening, they are, in many ways, universal. If age brings complaints, it also lends us perspective and wisdom. We all learn we must compromise, that no marriage is perfect, but that upon mature reflection, most of us feel grateful to have experienced the love another has granted us.

'Tequila Sunset' (McTell)
Written in California during what biographer Hockenhull refers to as McTell's 'hit hangover', this is a finely constructed song that has all the ingredients of a hit single: a catchy melody, confessional lyrics and a lovely, memorable chorus. Salvaged from an ill-fated collaboration with famous producer Shel Talmy, it illustrates a temporary fix to long-term problems. Words are not what's needed at the moment ('whatever we say, it's just the booze talking'); they are rather a means to (in the words of another famous songwriter) get them through the night. Numerous lyrical details complement the main narrative. The fact that 'skinny dogs howl at a Mexico moon' while shoeless children roam streets full of dreams serves to remind the narrator that his emotional struggles, while quite real, pale next to more practical concerns. Effective backing vocals and light orchestration fill out the sound of the track. It's unclear whether The Eagles' 1973 hit, 'Tequila Sunrise', influenced McTell, but it's probable. McTell has confessed it's his favourite song on the album and this listener agrees.

Above: 'My desire is to communicate my views of life and experience through songs'. (*Ralph May*)

Left: After his father abandoned the family, McTell faced a difficult childhood. (*Ralph May*)

Right: 'When you trade your name for a number and a uniform of brown'. McTell as a member of the Queen's Surrey Regiment, 1960. (*Ralph May*)

Right: 'It was the guitar that led me to write songs'. (*Ralph May*)

Below: Wizz Jones was an important early influence on McTell. (*Copyright-free image by Tony1212 licensed under CC BY-SA 4.0*)

Left: Unusually, the cover of McTell's first album, *Eight Frames A Second,* included neither its title nor the artist's name. (*Transatlantic*)

Right: This early poster reflects the drawing power of McTell's ragtime guitar pieces. (*Ralph May*)

Right: Peter Thaine's colourful cover illustration for *Spiral Staircase* hints at the many challenges faced by the narrator of the album's title track. (*Transatlantic*)

Left: Thaine's Victorian cover for *My Side Of Your Window* portrays three characters who feature in tracks from the album. (*Transatlantic*)

Left: The brooding nature of the album's cover signals the new direction McTell was ready to take on ***You Well Meaning Brought Me Here***. (***Famous***)

Right: 'Streets Of London', McTell's most famous composition, has been covered by more than 200 artists. (***Ralph May***)

Right: 'First Song', 'Sylvia' and 'Barges' are among the standout tracks on McTell's fifth album, *Not Till Tomorrow*. (*Reprise*)

Left: Enrique Serra Y Auque's imaginative painting serves as the cover for *Easy*, one of McTell's best-selling albums. (*Reprise*)

Left: McTell's pose on the cover of the highly successful *Streets* album was inspired by a photo of American musician Georgia Tom. (*Warner Bros.*)

Right: Though not as popular as the albums that preceded it, *Right Side Up* is one of McTell's strongest releases. (*Warner Bros.*)

McTell met Nanna Stein in 1965 in Paris. They have been together ever since. (*Ralph May*)

Right: The 1979 album *Slide Away The Screen* finds McTell in a bit of a holding pattern. (*Warner Bros.*)

Left: *Water Of Dreams* features two strong protest songs, including the title track and 'Bentley And Craig'. (*Leola*)

Right: McTell's song 'Hands Of Joseph' was inspired by the Bahamian guitarist Joseph Spence. (*Copyright-free image by Eric Parker licensed under CC BY-NC 2.0*)

Left: Numerous members of Fairport Convention contributed to *Bridge Of Sighs*, a strong McTell album released in 1987. (*Leola*)

Right: A biography of the Welsh poet Dylan Thomas inspired McTell to record *The Boy With A Note*, an evocation of the artist's tumultuous life. (*Leola*)

Left: Bass player Danny Thompson has appeared on numerous McTell recordings. (*Copyright-free image by beanmunster licensed under CC BY 2.0*)

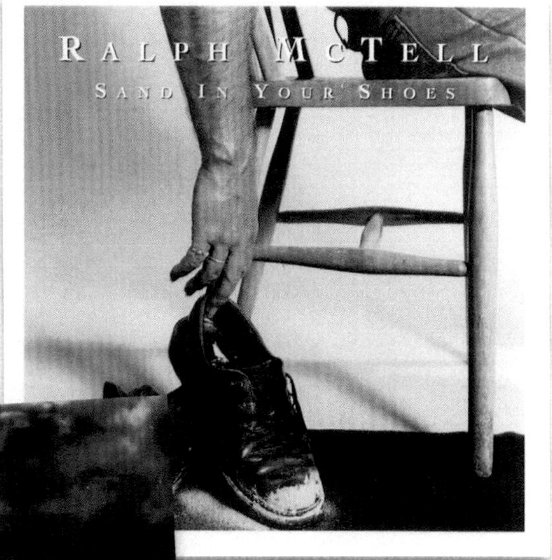

Right: *Sand In Your Shoes* is the work of a mature artist, thoroughly conversant with his gift. (*Transatlantic*)

Left: McTell's longest album, *Red Sky* is largely dour in tone but includes some of his strongest compositions. (*Leola*)

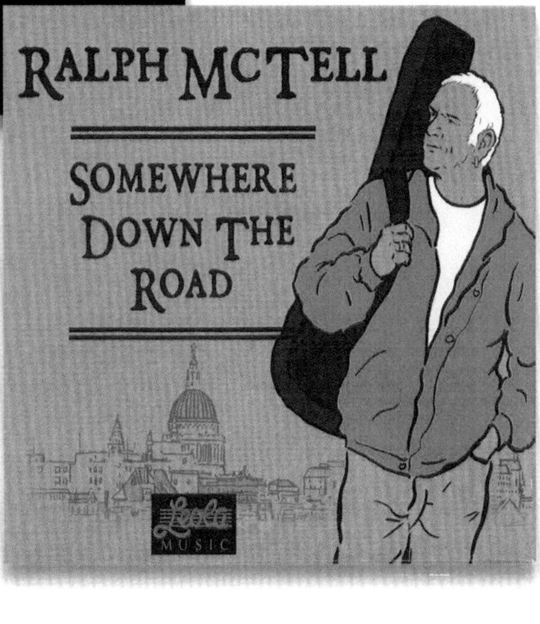

Right: In 2010, McTell released *Somewhere Down The Road*, his first album of original songs in ten years. (*Leola*)

Left: *Sofa Noodling* is an informal, engaging collection of instrumentals. (*Leola*)

Right: The title of McTell's 2019 studio album *Hill Of Beans* was inspired by a line from the 1942 film *Casablanca*. (*Leola*)

Left: McTell's love of the country blues is on full display on *Blue Skies, Black Heroes*, a collection of covers. (*Leola*)

Right: Blind Boy Fuller's recordings, often featuring a National resonator guitar, were McTell's inspiration to record *National Treasure*. (*Leola*)

Above: A wonderful live album that showcases the breadth of McTell's repertoire, *Ralph Albert & Sydney* features performances from concerts in London and Sydney, Australia. (*Warner Bros.*)

Right: In 2006, David Suff assembled a box set, *The Journey*, that includes numerous rare tracks and studio favourites. (*Leola*)

Above: Craig Ledoux's artwork highlights one of McTell's best tracks: 'From Clare To Here'. (*Craig Ledoux*)

Right: The author and McTell after his concert at the Ingleton Folk Festival in 2004. (*Paul O. Jenkins*)

Above: While he is pragmatic and recognises life's challenges, many of McTell's songs reflect his innate optimism.

Right: McTell outside Dylan Thomas's favorite pub, Brown's Hotel, in Laugharne, Wales in 2016. (*Eduardo Barroso Barreira*)

Above: Gordon Williams's digital collage interpretation of 'The Fairground' captures the sense of wonder felt by the song's narrator. (*Gordon Williams*)

'Weather The Storm' (McTell)

On his website, McTell relates that he based this inspiring song on the experiences of a friend who had just emerged from a harrowing separation. A wonderfully universal piece, its chorus acknowledges the challenges we all face but stresses life's ultimate reward. McTell cleverly doesn't describe the exact cause of the struggle, simply using the pronoun, 'it'. If the lyrics are profoundly simple and direct, it is the singing that carries the day here. McTell's heartfelt vocal performance is skillfully and powerfully abetted by the contributions of backup singers Tony Rivers, Ken Gold and John Perry. It's no wonder that 'Weather The Storm' has remained one of McTell's most requested concert pieces and that one McTell devotee has given his website the same title.

'River Rising Moon High' (McTell)

Hypnotic in nature, this song's production is beautiful, with Danny Thompson's bass prominently on display. During his long career, Thompson was a member of the well-known folk group Pentangle and also played with the likes of Richard Thompson and John Martyn. After McTell met him in 1968, the maestro of the double bass was nearly always included in the line-up when it was time to go into the studio. Another lush, gorgeously produced track, 'River Rising' is the type of number that makes a welcome earworm.

'From Clare To Here' (McTell)

Besides 'Streets Of London', this is McTell's most famous and enduring composition and has been covered by dozens of performers, including The Fureys and Nanci Griffith. Often mistaken for a traditional Irish folk song, or at least the product of an Irish composer, it stems from an incident in McTell's life. When he was employed on a building site in 1963, McTell sensed the loneliness of one of his fellow labourers, a shy young Irishman named Michael, and struck up a friendship with him. One day, after McTell remarked how strange it must be for a rural lad like him to be working in London, Michael uttered the phrase that lends the song its name: 'yeah, it's a long way from Clare to here'. So many elements of man's existence are slyly inserted into the short piece. We listen to the homesick young man touch upon the guilt of missing mass and not writing often enough to his mother, the difficulty of maintaining good relationships in crowded housing and the consolation of drink. Added to these insights into human needs is a good deal of poetry.

> I sometimes hear a fiddle play
> Or maybe it's a notion
> I dream I see white horses dance
> Upon that other ocean.

The song's production is powerful but also appropriately muted. The traditional Irish sounds of a harp and whistle lightly augment McTell's guitar and vocals.

'Chairman And The Little Man' (McTell)

Another track about foreign lands follows, although it is vastly different in nature and tone. After watching a documentary about China on TV, McTell was inspired to write a song about the guileless affection workers seemed to feel for Chairman Mao. There is a certain edge to McTell's lyrics, however, that expresses discontentment. Hockenhull (90) has cleverly noted that the song might serve an additional purpose of hinting 'at the struggle between artist and big business'. At times, McTell did struggle to please various record label heads and, together with his brother Bruce, eventually established his own label, Mays Records, in 1981. McTell (Awde 184): 'We knew we had some sort of market and I just let him make the decisions and we went along with it... It was an acknowledgement that having given it a shot in the commercial sense, it was the final proof that we would have to do it our way if we were going to continue to do it'.

'Country Boys' (McTell)

This song celebrates what Americans call 'good old boys' and is based on oppositions of country and city, night and morning. If a minor element of the McTell canon, its gentle electric backing track is well executed and the chorus is catchy. A slightly different version is included on the CD release of the *Streets* album, for which the recording was originally intended.

'Slow Burning Companion' (McTell)

This ode to the consolations of a good smoke remains a favourite of its composer. McTell (official website): 'In my mind, this particular 'midnight station' is to be found in Rugby. I spent many hours there smoking little hand-rolled fuses of time waiting for that last train back to London. These were during my folk club days, but that place and those shadows are with me still'. Excellent harmonies contribute to the feel of the piece.

'Nightmares' (McTell)

A track recorded in one take, this song features Pick Withers (of later Dire Straits fame) on drums. To this listener, the meaning is somewhat elusive. McTell has mentioned that his intention here was to highlight a fact with which almost every female listener would be familiar: how men struggle to verbalise their feelings. The lyrics, expressed in the form of a conversation, seem to convey that we must confront our fears (as given life in our dreams) but also that, like nightmares, such anxieties will pass.

'May You Never' (Martyn)

An album that began with a cover is bookended by another, one of John Martyn's most well-known compositions, also covered by Eric Clapton on his *Slowhand* album released a year after *Right Side Up*. McTell has sometimes been compared to Martyn (1948-2009) and, indeed, they share some characteristics. Both possessed exceptional guitar skills, were gifted songwriters and began as folkies before eventually branching out into additional musical genres.

Slide Away The Screen (1979)

Personnel:
Ralph McTell: guitar, piano, banjo, harmonica, vocals
Dave Pegg: guitar, bass
Mick Weaver: piano, organ
Martin Jenner: guitar, steel guitar
Nigel Portman-Smith: bass
Dave Mattacks: drums, percussion
Telephone Bill: backing vocals
Jerry Donahue: guitar
Robert Kirby: piano, electric piano
Phil Palmer: guitar
John Mealing: organ, synthesizer
Mike Piggott: fiddle
Simon Nicol: guitar
Richard Thompson: guitar
John Kirkpatrick: accordion on 'Save The Last Dance For Me'
Recorded at Chipping Norton Studios.
Produced by Dave Pegg.
UK release date: April 1979
Highest chart places: did not chart.
Running time: 46:04

At this point in his career, McTell was hoping to create a folk-rock sound and the musicians he enlisted for the project are certainly first-rate. But if the dozen songs gathered together here sound just fine, few of them rise to the quality of McTell's earlier work in terms of either lyrics or melodies. Dave Pegg's production is thoughtful and attractive throughout, but the material seems to find the artist in a bit of a holding pattern. The cover depicts a silhouetted figure opening a cast-iron screen gate, sliding away a screen. The metaphor for discovery, honesty and openness is apparent.

In her review for *Record Mirror*, Susan Kluth characterises the album's songs as less personal than those on *Right Side Up* and praises the fact that McTell's maturity has resulted in compositions that are broader and more detached than many of his earlier efforts. Writing for *Allmusic.com*, Chris Woodstra states that the album 'represents one of McTell's finest recorded moments'.

'Love Grows' (McTell)

Dedicated to his sons, Tom and Billy, the opening track traces the evolution of love from first kisses to the 'arrival of some little stranger' and makes clear that becoming parents increases the bond between partners. Two riddles underline the point: 'What is it the more that you divide it/It just comes back multiplied?' and 'What is it the more you give away/The more it seems to come your way?' Written in McTell's mid-thirties, this is a song of a mature man and happy parent who seems intent on letting others in on the secret he has discovered. McTell was pleased with the sound offered by a new 12-string guitar he used on the recording and the arpeggiated lilt on display here is lovely. The song showcases the best of pop production, featuring numerous piano fills and effective backing vocals. This listener believes the song's qualities are such that it could have been a hit single.

'One Heart' (McTell)
The album's second track is a straightforward love song that echoes Elmore James' 'It Hurts Me Too' and features an intriguing guitar solo by Jerry Donahue. The comparative blandness of the lyrics is all too typical of the album. Perhaps the listener has become spoilt by previous McTell gems.

'Gold In California' (McTell)
Originally composed in 1972 on piano, McTell reworked this piece during his sojourn in California but was never completely satisfied with the recorded track. Listening to the song makes it clear that, like other prospectors who travelled to the Golden State, McTell did not discover its promised riches. His mention of Paul on the Damascus road in the third verse is intriguing. In Acts Nine, Saul, who had fiercely persecuted the followers of Jesus, is blinded by a heaven-sent light, reverses course and eventually, as Paul, becomes an influential apostle. Via his frequent mention of the sun in the piece, McTell picks up the light imagery and observes how near one is to experiencing a similar conversion.

'Van Nuys (Cruise Night)' (McTell)
As close as McTell comes to a rock track, 'Van Nuys' is an atmospheric piece that captures the essence of a Los Angeles neighbourhood known for romantic car rides under the cover of night. While McTell's efforts to expand his more typical folk-pop style often do not come off, this composition works and features a radio-friendly chorus. McTell's atypical vocal approach reminds this listener of James Taylor's 'I Was Only Telling a Lie'.

'London Apprentice' (McTell)
Not to be confused with a song that McTell would later include on his *Somewhere Down The Road* album, this very brief instrumental is pleasant but not intriguing.

'Traces' (McTell)
McTell bares his heart in a passionately delivered love song of recognition, reminiscence and regret. A Proustian whiff of perfume sets its narrator's mind reeling back to a past love, one who made him feel passion's peaks and valleys as no other had before or has since. A quiet, reflective song on which

McTell accompanies himself on piano, it is brief and to the point. Surely it speaks to an emotion almost every one of us has felt. We can be content in our present relationship and yet still be rocked by memories of a past love not willingly brought to mind. McTell's ability to evoke a response from his listeners is readily apparent in this song.

'Heroes & Villains' (McTell)
McTell observes in his liner notes that this is 'a song to suggest that even the blackest moments may have a positive outcome'. Once more, the composer approaches his topic by exploring dualities: the heroes and villains of the title, comedies and tragedies, lies and truths, right roads and wrong turns. The track's synthesiser solo places it squarely in 1979.

'Harry (Don't Go)' (McTell)
This engaging, Calypso-tinged song is dedicated to a roadie from Guyana who worked on the tour that followed the release of McTell's *Streets* album and later dedicated himself to helping the elderly.

'Autumn' (McTell)
In 2005, McTell released *Time's Poems*, a complete collection of his lyrics to date. The songs are organised not by title or chronologically but rather by seasons. McTell is quite attuned to the varying natures of the four seasons and has observed that there are fewer songs devoted to autumn than to winter, summer or spring. In a very quiet, very short track, McTell explores the cycle of the seasons but ends by admitting that autumn still leaves him feeling blue.

'Promises' (McTell)
Here, the narrator reassures the object of his love that although promises are all too easy to make, he will stand by his commitment 'Till the desert brings forth fruit/Till romance gives way to truth'. On 'Words I Couldn't Say' from the *Bridge Of Sighs* album, he will return to the theme, stating that although such conventional phrases may seem tired, they are sometimes necessary.

'White Dress' (Swarbrick/McTell)
This piece was adapted from Fairport Convention fiddler Dave Swarbrick's original composition dedicated to vocalist Sandy Denny and included on the group's 1975 album, *Rising For The Moon*. While Denny sings much of the song in the first person, McTell's version shifts to the second person. McTell has stated that he sees the image of the titular white dress as a means to reunite a couple that has been on the outs. A few well-timed orchestral flourishes and a tasty guitar solo highlight a strong performance of a well-written song.

'Save The Last Dance For Me' (Pomus/Shuman)
The fact that McTell chose to include this cover may have contributed to a growing perception by some that he had lost a certain edge and that his sound was worryingly creeping towards middle-of-the-road.

Tracks Included on the 1994 CD release of Slide Away the Screen:
'Banjo Man' (McTell)
McTell wrote this in honour of Stephen Wade (b. 1953), an American banjo player. The lyrics describe how music can ease our worries and make life more palatable. McTell delights in taking the opportunity to display his own banjo skills.

'Trouble I'm In' (McTell)
This track is an indictment of the dangers of dissipation, its bluesy performance hearkening back to some of McTell's earliest recordings.

'Wish I Could Pray' (McTell)
An echo in some ways of 'Mrs. Adlam's Angels', this song explores the consolation faith can bring but has proven elusive in McTell's life. Later rerecorded in a much fuller version for the 2019 release, *Hill Of Beans*.

'I'm Looking Over My Shoulder for You' (McTell)
A variation on the old blues convention of a man on the lookout for a scorned lover that sounds a bit like Lynyrd Skynyrd.

'If I Don't Get Home' (McTell)
Here, McTell delivers a confession that applies to almost every travelling musician. The sparse arrangement (McTell accompanies himself on the piano) lends to its moving intimacy.

Water Of Dreams (1982)

Personnel:
Ralph McTell: guitar, harmonium, electric piano, harmonica, mandolin, vocals
Liam Og O'Flynn: uilleann pipes on 'Water Of Dreams'
Gerry Conway: drums
Phil Collins: drums
Dave Pegg: bass
Billy Livsey: piano, synthesizer
Neil Ardley: keyboards on 'England'
Phil Palmer: guitar
Richard Thompson: guitar
Bill Lovelady: nylon guitar
Albert Lee: guitar on 'Please Don't Haunt Me'
Steve Simpson: piano accordion on 'Got To Be With You'
Howard Evans: trumpet on 'Geordie's On The Road'
Leah May: backing vocals on 'England'
Prelude: backing vocals
Recorded at Essex Studios
Produced by Ralph McTell and Martin Levan.
Released in 1982
Highest chart places: did not chart.
Running time: 42:20

While it must also have felt somewhat dispiriting, McTell felt enormous relief upon being released from his big label contract with Warner Bros. And while it contains a few undistinguished tracks, *Water Of Dreams* is a marked improvement on its predecessor and shows the benefits of artistic liberation. Assisted by Martin Levan, McTell again serves as producer and lends tasteful and understated nuance to many selections.

Mixed in with a few pieces that explore varying aspects of love, McTell includes two of his best protest songs here ('Bentley And Craig' and the title track). Mostly, however, the album is one of tributes. McTell celebrates an artist (Joseph Spence), resilient lads from the north of England and an old friend. In some ways, the protest songs can also be seen in this light, celebrating, as they do, young men who have suffered injustice. Finally, the addition of 'England' to the CD release of the album finds McTell paying tribute to his homeland in grand fashion. The cover photo depicts a smiling, relaxed McTell.

'Got To Be With You' (McTell)
The album opens with a solid folk rock track that features prominent bass, McTell's harmonica and Steve Simpson's piano accordion. McTell wrote the piece for a Norwegian woman he knew who had made many changes to her life in hopes of finding love.

'Please Don't Haunt Me' (McTell)
An atmospheric tune highlighted by Albert Lee's lead guitar demonstrates how much McTell still loved the blues. The song's theme is similar in some ways to *Slide Away The Screen*'s 'Traces', but is much darker and sinister in nature.

'I'm Not A Rock' (McTell)
By its very title, this track may remind listeners of Paul Simon's 'I Am a Rock', while a line from the second verse, 'just some shelter from the storm', brings Dylan to mind. The song is an honest response to a friend who continually leans on the narrator, demanding emotional support but often offering little in return. McTell's harmonica work is front and centre here, reminding us of how proficient he is on the pocket piano.

'Hands Of Joseph' (McTell)
After being introduced by friend Gary Petersen to the Bahamian guitarist Joseph Spence (1910-1984), McTell chose to pay tribute to both his life and his musicianship in this excellent song. The lyrics gracefully demonstrate how Spence embodied American trial lawyer Louis Nizer's (1902-1994) famous quotation: 'a man who works with his hands is a labourer; a man who works with his hands and his brains is a craftsman; but a man who works with his hands and his brain and his heart is an artist'. The line, 'He's happy all the time', namechecks the title of Spence's 1964 album and 'While the rolling sea got mad' is inspired by one of his most famous pieces, 'Out On The Rolling Sea'. Finally, the lengthy instrumental passage that concludes the track pays tribute to the Bahamian's distinctive style and is based on Spence's 'Great Dreams From Heaven'. McTell was delighted to be invited to participate in Fred Ferguson's 2021 documentary on Spence, *Joseph Spence: The Virtuoso From Small Hope*. He is interviewed throughout the piece and is quoted as saying, 'I felt it's part of my job to write thank you notes in song to the people that have influenced me'. The impact of McTell's tribute is most apparent when, during the film, Spence's nephew is moved to tears upon listening to 'Hands Of Joseph'.

'Pykey Boy' (McTell)
'Pykey' or 'Pikey', used as a slang term for travellers, is now considered an offensive term by many in the UK. McTell's song, however, is written in tribute to the tremendous pluck, defiance and spirit shown by these people. McTell often saw travellers near his boyhood home and felt a certain affinity with them. Here, he celebrates their ability to embrace all aspects of life and to live in the moment, a lesson many contemporary urban dwellers spend hours studying. For listeners who might need it, here is a glossary: 'Gadjo' is a term for non-Romani people; 'juk' means dog; 'moosh' is a stranger; 'parni' is water and 'kuschty' means cool.

'Bentley & Craig' (McTell)

This moving song tells the story of Christopher Craig and Derek Bentley, two young men from McTell's native London suburb of Croydon who, in November 1952, tried to commit a robbery. A police officer was killed during the attempted arrest. 'We all knew that Christopher Craig had shot the policeman', McTell recounts in *Angel Laughter* (133), 'and some knew that Derek Bentley was epileptic and mentally about eight years old'. Key to the prosecution's case was Bentley's tragically ambiguous statement, 'let him have it, Chris', interpreted either as a plea for his friend to surrender the firearm or a suggestion that Craig should fire. Just 16, Craig was too young to be sentenced to death. Bentley, however, was hanged only a few months after the incident. McTell recounts his feelings at the time: 'Now the paper told me that Bentley was dead. In response to all my bewilderment and the awful silence that followed the news, all my voices were murmuring at the same time, and I begged for an answer with every look that I could give my family and the few grown-ups that we came into contact with'. An excellent protest song, it raised public awareness of the lingering injustice and may have contributed to Bentley being granted a full pardon in 1998 (a year after his sister, Iris Bentley, died), thus refuting the claim made in McTell's earlier 'I've Thought About It', that 'songs never change things'. The line, 'You can pardon Derek Bentley who never took a life', designates the composition as one that exemplifies R. Serge Denisoff's fifth type of protest song, one that 'proposes specific actions to solve real or imagined social problems'. English folk singer June Tabor includes a haunting version of McTell's song on her 1997 album, *Aleyn*. Elvis Costello's 'Let Him Dangle' (on his 1989 album *Spike*) also revisits the incident, though in a much different fashion.

'Water Of Dreams' (McTell)

The album's title track is reminiscent of the classic protest song, 'Joe Hill', via its use of a narrator who meets the spirits of three martyrs. Blair Peach is the major figure here. To most contemporary listeners, the name means nothing. Peach was a 33-year-old white teacher (born in New Zealand) who was killed while taking part in an anti-racism demonstration in London in April 1979. His death was a cause célèbre for a brief time; McTell's song was written to preserve his memory. Two figures who accompany Peach in the dream are Jimmy Kelly (who died shortly after being beaten by Liverpool police in 1979) and Liddle Towers (another victim of a police attack). This background is necessary to understand the first two verses. The real message of the song, though, comes in its chorus:

> If you can learn to live with your doubts
> You will soon learn to live with the lie,
> But the questions will rise on the water of dreams
> And be washed to the shore to be seen,
> By your sleeping eye.

This is McTell's direct appeal to the conscience of an apathetic public. McTell apparently includes himself in this group, for in the last verse, the three martyrs signify that it is precisely because he 'never did anything' that they are visiting him. By including himself among the guilty, McTell frees himself from the kind of self-righteousness that blunts the impact of many protest songs. One hopes that the track reached enough contemporary listeners to stir them to action, thus fulfilling one of Denisoff's identified roles for protest songs: 'to solicit outside support and sympathy for a cause'. The insertion of the uilleann pipes (played by the virtuoso Liam Óg O'Flynn, of Planxty fame) is nicely restrained and adds to the track's contemplative air.

'Affairs Of The Heart' (McTell)
Since McTell employed the same phrase for his 1989 compilation album, we know he rates the song. It is an earnest, fine performance that demonstrates the kind of honesty its composer admires in the genre of country music. The head/heart dichotomy employed in the song was famously explored by Thomas Jefferson in a 1786 letter now known as a 'Dialogue Between The Head And Heart', where the statesman reluctantly acknowledges the triumph of the former over the latter.

'Cold On The Stones' (McTell)
This song was inspired by an evening in which McTell and Bert Jansch were kicked out of a bar in New York. Its tone is defiant and the track features a very catchy chorus. Buried deep in the mix is McTell on mandolin.

'I Want You' (Dylan)
Bob Dylan had long been one of McTell's heroes by the time he covered this track from *Blonde On Blonde*. McTell's reading is much more gentle, controlled and subdued than the original and thus serves to highlight the differences between the two bards. While each wants to make an impression on his listeners, Dylan's approach is much more confrontational and forceful. He is not afraid to offend. If he is Malcolm X, McTell is Martin Luther King, Jr. seeking a more peaceful approach to effecting change.

'Geordie's On The Road' (McTell)
Another song that champions the underdog, 'Geordie's On The Road', was inspired by a young man McTell first met in America, who became a devoted fan and attended McTell's gigs whenever he visited Newcastle. The last verse ('May the road that leads you on/Like the choice to be alone/Be direction freely made/And at the right time lead you home') echoes the famous Irish blessing, 'may the road rise to meet you'. Stately horns and a lovely melody lend gravitas to the track. Grenfell astutely asserts that one message of the song is that to some, like this Geordie, 'stasis is death'.

'Song For Martin' (McTell)
Written for Martin 'Tubs' Sole, an old friend from McTell's busking days in Paris, this is a stirring emotional appeal to rally around a man in need (Sole fought a long battle against drug addiction). Like many in his situation, the title figure won't admit he needs a little help from his friends ('Now don't take it hard when he says he doesn't need you/'Cos that's when he needs you most'). Simple compassion and fellowship are stressed as McTell begins the chorus (and its first two verses) with a direct appeal: 'Don't leave Martin alone tonight'. In typical McTell fashion, the song has an optimistic spin to it, the chorus ending with the hope that 'This time I think he's coming through'. The fact that Sole later died in an accidental fire is somehow immaterial. The message of human solidarity is what survives. Graham Preskett's synth work is exceptional here and Phil Collins features on drums.

Tracks Included on the 2003 CD Release of Water of Dreams:
'Grey Sea Strand' (McTell)
This song is a moving tale of the residual guilt felt by a man after he was unable to save his brother from drowning. McTell was inspired to write it after hearing the real-life events in Donegal from a friend, Jim McCann (1944-2015), of Dubliners fame. The story begins by showing us a young girl walking to a strand. In an introduction to a live performance of the song, McTell notes that the little girl is 'one of the brothers' young daughter'. By her side, holding her hand, walks a 'big man'. They move towards the water to revisit the scene of his brother's accidental drowning. Such have been the repercussions of the event that the grieving adult now seeks solace from the young girl. The second verse shows the big man drinking, staring out the rain-streaked windows down to the water. We quickly learn why he is so haunted by the event. The brothers were tossed overboard in a gale and the non-swimming brother had urged the big man to let him go so that 'at least one shall be saved'. His brother's self-sacrifice has left the big man feeling the guilt of the survivor. So overcome was he by his brother's selfless act that rescuers later found him swimming the wrong way from the land as if unable to face life without his brother, unwilling to continue living if his brother could not. The first two verses are repeated at the song's conclusion, suggesting that the survivor has been unable to move on, to rejoin life. His life is now one of repeated drinking and grieving, of being led about instead of leading as was once his custom. The compassionate little girl, representing resilient youth, has become his emotional crutch. As his career progressed, McTell began to compose and perform an increasing number of songs on the piano and the sparse keyboard accompaniment employed here complements the track's tone.

'England' (McTell)
Based on a series of rhetorical questions, 'England' finds McTell examining the roots of patriotism. McTell (Hockenhull 100): 'I wanted a song that could

be appreciated and enjoyed by anyone, whatever their ethnic background, who was born here'. Hockenhull (101) notes some echoes of Rupert Brooke's poem, 'The Soldier'. Though it was originally released as a single in 1981, many urged McTell to rerelease the song after the Falkland Isles war in 1982 in order to ride the wave of patriotism then current. But in his lyrics ('Don't make this out to be a battle hymn or song of victory') McTell has, in a sense, anticipated such exploitation. He declined the offer, spurning an opportunity to possibly gain a second hit single in order to retain his self-respect as an artist. The song's production is a bit heavy-handed and thus blunts its impact. The modern sound of the synthesiser is out of place here and the use of the children's chorus, if endearing, is just slightly too sweet.

Bridge Of Sighs (1987)

Personnel:
Ralph McTell: guitar, piano, synthesiser, vocals
Alun Davies: guitar
Maartin Allcock: bass
Gerry Conway: drums
Jerry Donahue: guitar
Graham Preskett: keyboards, violin
Benny Gallagher: backing vocals
Simon Nicol: guitar on 'Mr. Connaughton'
Dave Swarbrick: violin on 'Mr. Connaughton'
Richard Thompson: guitar
Geraint Watkins: accordion
Dave Pegg: bass
Tom Keane: uilleann pipes on 'The Setting'
Danny Thompson: double bass
Brian Robson: piano
Sam Mitchell: National steel guitar on 'Something The Matter With Mary'
Recorded at Raezor Studios, and Essex Studio
Produced by Ralph McTell
UK release date: January 1987
Running time: 46:58

McTell's first album of original songs in four years, *Bridge Of Sighs* represents a strong comeback. Difficulties with management, however, resulted in it receiving little fanfare upon release. A crack team of musicians was assembled for the sessions. These included current and former Fairport Convention members Simon Nicol, Gerry Conway, Dave Swarbrick, Richard Thompson and Dave Pegg. Maartin Allcock, adept on many instruments, also played a key role. Another key addition was Cat Stevens' former right-hand man, guitarist Alun Davies. While most of McTell's previous studio vocals had been recorded separately, on this album, they were captured live. The resulting immediacy adds greatly to the music's impact and overall feel.

The bridge has long served as an apt metaphor for uniting separated parties. Here, McTell presents us with numerous examples of people trying to connect on various levels. If these attempts vary in terms of success, they all serve to highlight McTell's keen understanding of the human condition and his ability to translate it into song. The original release features a colourful abstract cover, while the CD sports a painting by Jan Leman that rather ominously shows two men about to meet on a bridge.

'Throw Out A Line And Dream' (McTell)

Like many of the album's songs, the first track alternates between two different points of view. One party is optimistic, seeing a river, harbour and road, whereas the other sees only a stream, quay or track. The idealistic narrator pokes fun at himself by admitting that 'wise men sleep/It is fools who dream', but more important is his preference for freedom over possession ('You want 'em locked up/And I want 'em free'). The song establishes themes that will recur throughout the album: dreaming, optimism and communication and is typical in that it provides no resolution to the disagreements that riddle it.

'Mr. Connaughton' (McTell)
This track is a touching portrait of the man who briefly served as a sort of surrogate father to young Ralph May. Originally released as a B-side single in 1983, it reveals how the man helped the boy experience some of the typical father-son activities he would otherwise have missed, such as building a soapbox cart and fixing up a motorbike. Even more important, though, was the daily emotional presence of a man who radiated warmth and love, someone who helped a boy smile through days of gapped teeth and lonely anguish. Years later, McTell's memories are vague; questions are repeatedly asked of both the departed Mr. Connaughton and McTell's own memory ('were you from Cork or Tipperary?', 'was your first name Kevin or Mike?'). The details are secondary, though, the singer knows. No matter his first name, Mr. Connaughton, an optimistic man who 'laughed as often as not', played a role in McTell's life that he will never forget. Dave Swarbrick's subtle fiddle lends a beautiful touch to this moving composition. Years later, McTell was gratified to meet Mr. Connaughton's daughter after a concert, who let him know that her father had heard the song before passing. Robert Welshons wrote a short story based on the piece that was published in the *North American Review* in 2003.

'The Girl From The Hiring Fair' (McTell)
Though originally intended for Fairport Convention, this track has become a staple in McTell's repertoire. Danny Thompson's forceful bass introduction creates an atmosphere of tense anticipation while each verse brings the determined field hand closer to his dream girl. Though his attempts at verbal communication falter, the narrator's love is eventually realised via what can be called pure natural attraction. Indeed, by the song's end, his love won and the narrator thanks the stars for their assistance. Though he has never recorded it, McTell has written a sequel titled 'Crimea' that details the now-married man's experiences in the Crimean War (1853-1856).

'Choufleur' (McTell)
Here, the narrator's lover repeatedly tries to draw him out and help him share with her his problem. The caress of his French nickname (the rather unromantic 'cauliflower' in English) is her key communicative device and seems to succeed by coaxing a smile from him by the song's end. This dreamy slice of life again highlights Thompson's excellent bass work.

'Something The Matter With Mary' (McTell)
Again, a vague problem is explored. The narrator is frustrated with his inability to find a resolution and the song's beat mirrors his insistent questioning. While 'Choufleur' hints at a coming reconciliation, this piece fades out with clouds very much still on the horizon. The instrumental accompaniment is an excellent example of the successful folk-rock sound McTell is regularly able to achieve.

'Bridge Of Sighs' (McTell)
Richard Thompson's stinging guitar launches the album's title track, another 'you and me' song. As in 'Throw Out A Line', we are privy to an exchange of two differing points of view. The narrator acknowledges a problem but sees hope, represented by a bridge that can unite the two. There is 'no disgrace' in compromise, he claims, in trying to work things out. In fact, compromise is inevitable in life if you don't want to be consumed in its flames. We must meet on the bridge. Still, in the chorus, the narrator himself seems to doubt the value of compromise ('Does anyone get what they really wish?'). As is the case with so many of the songs on the album, things are left unresolved. Argumentative, duelling guitars exchange blows before fading away. McTell has performed the piece live with Fairport Convention on occasion, lending it a rock feel.

'The Setting' (McTell)
Even on an album of such strong material, 'The Setting' stands out. McTell has endorsed it as one of his most accomplished songs (20 May 2003 email to author): 'I'd just been reading some short stories by Sean O'Faolain and I realised at one point I was learning not about the central character in the story but about somebody else – in this case, the guy left behind. I just became intrigued by his unexplained history'. The beautiful, plaintive melody perfectly fits the message of the song. Yes, it is hard to leave behind what you know, but it is equally difficult to be the one left behind. By the song's end, the narrator is left to draw inspiration from nature's example, here the starlings, whose spirits are not dampened by the rain. Separation is a natural part of life, as natural as rain itself, but this message does little to lift the spirits of the brother left behind. Unlike the more fortunate narrator in 'The Girl From The Hiring Fair', to this man, the stars are hidden by rain clouds. Tom Cain's uilleann pipes hint at a setting typical for songs of emigration, Ireland. McTell later stated that he wished he hadn't referenced emigration here, since his stronger intention was to portray a moment. The English folk duo Show of Hands, brilliantly paired 'The Setting' with Pádraig Mac Cumhaill's 'Mary from Dungloe' on their 2001 *No Song To Sing* album.

'Little Actress' (McTell)
'Little Actress' describes the kind of person many of us have known, the one who must always hold centre stage, the one who reduces the rest of us to

bit players in their self-penned drama. Any true communication with such a person is difficult. The song was inspired by the wife of one of McTell's friends, though decorum precludes the author from providing more specific information.

'Bad Girl' (McTell)
Though similar in some ways to the preceding track, here, McTell's approach is more sympathetic. The narrator sees through the title character and makes continued distinctions between 'bad' and 'sad'. McTell based this portrait on an acquaintance whose numerous contrasts fascinated him.

'Holiday Romance' (McTell)
Though this is an individual portrait, McTell stresses the universality of the situation ('anyone can fall for a holiday romance') and reinforces the message by cleverly paraphrasing Dylan's famous line: 'ain't it just like a woman/ain't it just like a man'. The man met on holiday has become a dream-like figure to the woman, one with whom real communication is no longer possible. Thus, in some ways, this is yet another song of dualities.

'Dreams Of You' (McTell)
'Dreams Of You' employs a beautiful melody based on Bach's 'Jesu, Joy Of Man's Desiring' and describes many of the agonies separated lovers must endure. Indeed, one assumes that McTell was as preoccupied with the famous melody as the song's narrator is when he notes that his dreams are driving him crazy 'like an old tune that haunts me'. The first four verses find the narrator posing question after question to his distant beloved. How can he bear the separation? How can he hope to get any work done in her absence? If love is a good thing, then why does it hurt so much? The dream imagery of the chorus is neatly picked up in the final verse as the narrator reflects that just as both his dreams and the songs that accompany them will end with the coming of dawn, so, too, will he soon be back in his lover's arms again. Such optimism is typical of McTell and fits well with the soothing, lilting melody that graces the lyrics. Though McTell has stated that he was never entirely happy with it, the song rose to number 48 on the pop charts when released as a single in 1975.

'Words I Couldn't Say' (McTell)
'Words I Couldn't Say' closes the album and serves as McTell's last word on the challenges of human communication. Though he is reluctant to deal in clichés, the narrator realises that sometimes one must simply give in to romantic conventions in order to be pragmatic. If the language of love varies greatly from person to person, in order to have real meaning, romantic sentiments must be spoken by the right person at the right time in the right way.

The Boy With A Note (1992)

Personnel:
Ralph McTell: guitar, piano, electric piano, vocals
Maartin Allcock: bass, guitar, synthesisers, keyboards
Andy Findon: saxophone
Graham Preskett: piano, violin
Maggie Reilly: vocals on 'Caitlin's Dream'
Dave Mattacks: percussion
Bob Kingdom: narrator on 'The Certain Tide'
Nerys Hughes: narrator on 'No Grown Man's Land'
Recorded at Raezor Studios.
Produced by Ralph McTell and Graham Preskett
UK release date: 1992
Highest chart places: did not chart
Running time: 49:35

When this album was released in 1992, it had been five years since McTell had offered a collection of original songs for adults. Writer's block had set in. Much-needed inspiration appeared in the form of Constantine Fitzgibbon's 1965 biography of Welsh poet Dylan Thomas (1914-1953). McTell's album also has much in common with Thomas's own 1947 prose piece, 'Return Journey', where the adult explores his youth in an attempt to understand the present. In 'Sylvia', McTell had shown his affinity for and interest in troubled poets, and in Thomas's tumultuous life, he found some common ground. Each was haunted by early success followed by fallow periods and self-doubt. Each experienced the loneliness and homesickness occasioned by touring. Each was keenly aware of the dangers of fame and felt the pressure to move beyond stardom to what is now referred to as superstardom.

The Boy With A Note began life as a radio play for BBC 2. Intrigued by the fact that Thomas loved pulp detective fiction, McTell took a decided gamble and chose to supplement songs with spoken passages (not analysed individually below) designed to investigate Thomas's motivation and secrets. For the original radio play, actors were hired to read these passages, but on the album, McTell chose to perform them himself. Nerys Hughes voices the thematically central segment, 'No Grown Man's Land', while actor Bob Kingdom reprises his role as Dylan Thomas (performed for the 1990 stage show, 'Dylan Thomas: Return Journey') for the 'Certain Tide' section. Between the narrated sections and the songs, a vision of Thomas emerges as a charming and talented man, nonetheless, riddled with doubts. Also running through both is the motif of deception, both of self and others. Thus, the final product is best described as a concept album, a collection of pieces that explores a definite theme.

By and large, McTell's artistic gamble succeeds. Many of the songs are very good and the fascinating spoken passages reveal another side of McTell's literary gifts. McTell again chose to co-produce the album, this time enlisting the aid of Graham Preskett, who also plays piano and violin and composed the overture. The production might best be characterised as warm and intimate. The use of Maartin Allcock's synthesiser was a calculated risk due to the fact that the album is a period piece, but his contributions are rarely jarring.

One senses McTell knew that, after such a long absence, he needed to deliver the goods in grand fashion, and *The Boy With A Note* certainly does that. It will likely remain a landmark in the performer's career and indicates the uniqueness of his contributions to the musical world. In just under 50 minutes, it succeeds both as an evocation of a famous poet's life and a musical work that can stand on its own. The cover features the famous Augustus John portrait of Thomas, painted between 1937-38.

Steve Leggett's review of the album for *Allmusic.com* is mixed. He praises songs like 'Conundrum Of Time' and 'Summer Girls' but concludes that in taking on such an ambitious project, McTell may have bitten off more than he could chew. 'Unfortunately, as the poet Robinson Jeffers once said, it is hard to set fire to too much thought and, to amend that statement, it is even harder to sing about it. That's the problem here. It all sounds so ponderous in the end'. Still, he does laud the level of detail involved in the project and characterises Thomas's story as one worth telling. Sid Griffin's review for *Q Magazine* is more positive, noting that McTell successfully paints a human portrait of Thomas 'without resorting to parody, sentimentality or the creation of a competing myth'.

'Overture'

Since a rough translation of the Welsh name Dylan is 'son of the sea wave' or 'born from the ocean', it is appropriate that the first sound we hear is the gentle lapping of waves. Indeed, water imagery pervades the entire album.

'Narration: Meet The Detective' (McTell)

'Summer Girls' (McTell)

In the album's first song, the narrator outlines a scheme to entice an equally romantic girl by pretending to be a Yankee sailor boy. The plan works and the fraudulent young man is hardly distraught when the affair ends as the truth emerges. He has been treating love as a game all along. The song has a certain warmth and gentle humour about it and the listener harbours no ill will towards the deceiver. The album's main theme, deception, is thus immediately introduced.

'Narration: The Slim Lover' (McTell)

'Irish Girl' (McTell)

This song's omniscient narrator expresses concern about the more practical aspects of the poet's decision to marry Caitlin. Thomas required a good deal of mothering and though Caitlin, an artist herself in some ways, was not always comfortable with this role, she did supervise what domestic comforts the couple's meagre income could provide. The melody is engaging and Preskett's fiddle work evokes the Emerald Isle.

'Narration: The Fitzroy' (McTell)

'Slip-Shod Tap-Room Dance (Soho So What)' (McTell)
Though most comfortable in his native Wales, Thomas was obliged to go to London fairly regularly to make contacts in the literary world and meet with potential publishers. This raucous number portrays one of what became many evenings spent in dissipation in the west end of England's capital city. The somewhat repetitive nature of both the lyrics and the melody reinforces this pattern of behaviour.

'Narration: These Soho Streets' (McTell)

'Poem: No Grown Man's Land' (McTell)

'Narration: The Reprieve Of Home (Laugharne)' (McTell)

'Conundrum Of Time (Shouldn't You Be Dancing)' (McTell)
The best song on the album, 'Conundrum Of Time', is presented as a dialogue between Thomas and his wife and begins by describing their marriage as one 'soldered by wishes and dreams'. Dylan and Caitlin loved one another but were also acutely sensitive to the slights made by one other. Each knew just which buttons to push to hurt the other. Their frequent squabbles were usually followed by sweet reconciliations and these dualities are reflected well in the chorus.

> Shouldn't you be dancing?
> Shouldn't I make rhymes?
> There's music all around us
> In this conundrum of time.
> But there's so many notes now
> Please find a tune
> Please find the harmony
> Please find it soon.

In verses two and three, the battle is joined again: 'Well I think that I get lucid, but you say I just get loose'; You mimic my poem so I oafishly dance'. While Thomas's extraverted public persona is well known, fewer understand that he was filled with self-doubt and continually preoccupied with providing for his wife and family. His was the familiar artist's struggle to gain a livelihood while practising his trade. Caitlin, he hoped, might lend him some discipline. Alas, the necessary discipline and harmony proved elusive. Thomas died while on tour in America in 1953. His death derailed Caitlin, who spent the rest of her life searching vainly for an adequate substitute. Indeed, she titled her 1957 memoir *Leftover Life To Kill*. In a 30 May 2004 email to the author, McTell explained that the allusion to plumbing he employs is deliberate. 'The pressure created in this relationship might be too much for the joint that is only soldered with their wishes and dreams'.

'Milk For One (Storm In A Tea Cup)' (McTell)
A song that in some ways echoes 'Summer Lightning' in its desire for domestic harmony, 'Milk For One' differs from the earlier tune in that it is set not before bedtime but rather on the morning after another quarrelsome evening. Another echo is the use of the song's subtitle. Like summer lightning, a storm in a teacup is an idiom for a basically insignificant event whose importance has been exaggerated. Thomas's offer to take his morning beverage black since milk is scarce is a sacrifice that indicates his willingness to take the first step towards making amends.

'Narration: Leaving For The States' (McTell)

'A Wonderful Country (A Proposition Of Prepositions)' (McTell)
This track reflects many of the feelings McTell experienced while on tour in America and its theme is also similar in some ways to 'If I Don't Get Home'. Besides including a good many prepositions, the song also adheres to a strict parallel structure in both its chorus and verses.

'Caitlin's Dream (Summer Birds Are Leaving)' (McTell)
If Thomas was a romantic, so was his wife. She also saw herself as a failed artist, a dancer who was not dancing. Here, her jealousy of Thomas's success is juxtaposed with everyday details of the domestic life she must endure in order to allow her husband the freedom to ply his trade, be it in England, America or even Czechoslovakia, where Thomas was invited to speak in 1949. The number is sensitively performed by Scottish singer Maggie Reilly (b.1956), best known for her work with Mike Oldfield.

'Narration: The Certain Tide' (McTell)

'Narration: Continuing Investigations' (McTell)

'Get Me A Doctor' (McTell)
Set to a melody similar to 'Hands Of Joseph', the country western instrumentation employed for this short track feels slightly out of place. Always constitutionally fragile, Thomas's dissipated lifestyle gradually took

its toll on his health. While on tour in America, things worsened. Perhaps the song's most significant line is, 'Get me a doctor/Not one who'll give me dope'. Like Hank Williams' demise earlier the same year and Elvis' death in 1977, Thomas's end in 1953 seems to have been caused as much by ill-advised prescriptions and shots as it was by existing conditions or abuse of alcohol.

'Narration: The Tunnels "Never End" In Sight' (McTell)

'I Miss You Most Of All' (McTell)
McTell studied Thomas's life thoroughly before writing the songs for this album. Dozens of Thomas's letters to Caitlin have been published and here, the composer amalgamates their essence. In this genuinely moving piece, McTell stacks a litany of missed opportunities before resolving the tension thus created with the simplest of statements: 'darling, I miss you most of all'.

'Narration: Naked At The Station' (McTell)

'Cradled In The Rocking Boat' (McTell)
As Grenfell has astutely observed (73), McTell chose to conclude the album not with Thomas's death but rather with a 'meditation on life'. Thomas never fully emotionally matured. In many ways, he remained 'the boy with a note' imprisoned and stunted by 'wild dreams of his own'. Such dreams made him a famous poet, but they did not make him a happy man. McTell first dwells on childhood scenes from Thomas's beloved Cwmdonkin Park in Swansea before adroitly transitioning to images from the estuary in Laugharne, Dylan's final home, where the poet beheld the unvarying, inevitable 'pull of the tide' that would transport him into an adult world he could never fully navigate. The project comes full circle with a reprise of the sound of lapping waves included in the overture. McTell's use of boat imagery is found throughout his work, including 'The Ferryman', 'Grey Sea Strand', 'Hands Of Joseph', 'The Islands', 'Tous Les Animaux Sont Tristes', 'Barges' and 'Lunar Lullaby'.

Sand In Your Shoes (1995)

Personnel:
Ralph McTell: guitar, keyboards, harmonica, vocals
Maartin Allcock: guitars, bass, accordion, keyboards, mandolin, bouzar, uilleann pipes, big drum, backing vocals
Gerry Conway: drums
Alun Davies: guitar
Jerry Donahue: guitar
Frank Gallagher: fiddle, whistles
Chris Leslie: violin, viola
Dave Pegg: bass
Guy Barker: trumpet
Chris Laurence: string bass
Graham Preskett: piano
Ralph Salmins: drums
Phil Todd: saxophone, clarinet
Leah May: backing vocals
Phil Beer: backing vocals
Steve Knightley: backing vocals
Mark Hopkin: backing vocals
Mevagissey Male Choir: vocals on 'The Enemy Within'
Recorded at Woodworm Studio, Raezor Studio
Produced by Maartin Allcock and Ralph McTell
UK release date: 1995
US release date: 1998
Highest chart places: did not chart
Running time: 67:47

Sand In Your Shoes is the work of a mature artist at the height of his powers, one who is at peace with himself and thus free to explore at length a variety of societal and personal issues. By far McTell's longest album to date, nearly half of its selections are five minutes or longer. Six of them can be classified as protest songs and yet the album has a gentleness to it, thanks largely to the warmth of McTell's voice and the muted approach to production. If the compositions display grave concerns, they do not pontificate. McTell has experienced enough of life to acknowledge its nuances and is wise enough to know that reasoned argument is ultimately more effective than aimless shouting. Perhaps 'thoughtful' is the best single word to describe this thought-provoking collection of compositions. The cover photograph shows a man's hands either reaching for or having just dropped a pair of well-heeled (and possibly sand-filled) shoes.

In his review for *Allmusic.com*, William Ruhlmann makes note of McTell's interest in 'the passage of time, the approach of death and several social concerns. The overall tone of the collection is elegiac, the songs full of loss and regret'. Ruhlmann is full of praise for the protest pieces included and summarises the album as a 'full, expansive collection of songs that makes a worthy addition to the singer/songwriter's catalogue'. Writing for *Q Magazine*, John Bauldie's review is mixed. He believes 'The Enemy Within' and 'Care In The Community' merely 'stumble towards coherence' and that McTell's efforts to 'grapple with big themes' are not always successful. He finds 'Jesus Wept' and 'Peppers And Tomatoes' better, and calls 'Still In Dreams' the album's simplest, but best song.

'Tous Les Animaux Sont Tristes' (McTell)
An intriguing portrait of loneliness, power and control, the album's opening track was inspired by the Greek shipping magnate, Aristotle Onassis. McTell (Hockenhull 151):

> Like many wealthy men, he believed he could acquire happiness and almost 'acquired' an artistic talent like Maria Callas because he hadn't anything else to do with his money. I think what happened to poor Callas, 'the small brown bird', was that she relieved the ache and the emptiness in his life, but in the end, it wasn't enough, and the 'silver arrow' is a metaphor for money and neglect. He metaphorically killed her, and then his darkness returned and he was still alone, so basically, as he couldn't get himself enough power, he married the widow of the most powerful man in the world.

The title phrase (translated as 'all animals are sad after making love'), McTell continues, 'comes from a line in a Latin play or poem, my friend Graham Preskett informs me, but I first heard it in French... Making love involves a climax and a subsequent anti-climax, which I equate with the young chap who's never satisfied'. The original reference is 'Omne animal post coitum triste'. Another way to regard the song is as an example of the age-old theme of innocence and experience. The goal, so long desired and romanticised during innocence, tastes far less sweet once realised.

'The Islands' (McTell/Allcock)
Maartin Allcock asked McTell to write something about the 1993 wreck of the oil tanker *Braer* off the Shetland Islands and the resulting environmental damage it caused. Chris Leslie's beautiful violin work accents the gentle warning McTell sounds in the song. Nature controlled the damage this time around, but we are left to wonder if we will be so lucky next time. 'The Islands' again demonstrates McTell's deft touch with protest material. Fairport Convention covered it on their 1995 *Jewel In The Crown* album.

'Fear Of Flying' (McTell)
Though shorter and less profound in scope, 'Fear Of Flying' revisits some of the same themes first explored in 'The Ferryman'. It is a rumination on life's journeys, not its destinations. The gentle nature of the piece indicates McTell's

stability; he is one who has learned to put aside his fears in order to 'reach out for the stars'.

'Care In The Community' (McTell)

Here, McTell revisits a theme first explored in 'Michael In The Garden', the general public's apathy towards and misunderstanding of the mentally challenged. In the song, we meet a probable schizophrenic, a disturbed woman talking endlessly to herself, a prostitute and a young man holding 'a one-sided conversation'. Before and after being introduced to this cast of societal misfits, we are reminded of how the more fortunate among us address the situation, or, rather, do not address it. The wonderful punning of the expression 'take care' used in the chorus, clearly signals McTell's intent to use the song as a warning. A society without compassion can quickly become one that is dangerous for all of its citizens. In this respect, 'Care In The Community' also mirrors 'Streets Of London'. McTell has stated (Hockenhull 146) that the song 'is basically about the way this country treats its less fortunate. It's a euphemism for abandonment and an attempt to say "Enough"'.

'I Don't Think About You' (McTell)

This swinging, country-flavoured track is addressed to an unnamed figure from the narrator's past. We think he doth protest too much. In fact, the song can be seen as an attempt to conjure a positive from a great many negatives. A tightly structured composition, each of its five verses employs a similar opening to reinforce the constant nature of the loved one's presence. She is in his thoughts each day, each night, each morning, each evening, each month. In verse four, the narrator admits that he retains hope that she might still change her mind and return to him, but rather than bemoan her absence, he seems cheerfully resigned to the fact that their separation is final. The melody and vocal delivery are similarly upbeat. This is a song of a mature man who recognises the folly of his continued hope but who also delights in its retention. The chorus supports this notion by negating the hope raised in each of the verses. The repetition and final denial of each hope listed in the final chorus confirm the narrator's mental health:

> But when I put it this way
> I can truly say
> That I don't wait
> And I don't dream
> And I don't think
> About you.

'The Enemy Within (The Band)' (McTell)

Still another protest song, 'The Enemy Within' turns Margaret Thatcher's phrase about the striking miners of 1984 against her. McTell cleverly chooses a member of the colliery band as the narrator. Numerous books have been written on the place of music in labour movements and the fact that a pamphlet is usually only read once but that a song can be sung repeatedly. Just as important as the message can be the effect it has on workers' morale. This portrayal of eroding hope is set to a wonderfully plaintive melody, complete with appropriate brass accompaniment. McTell's description of the abandoned band room as an echo of the miners' souls is another example of his poetic gift. All in all, a wonderful recording.

'Sand In Your Shoes' (McTell)

A chance remark by McTell's brother Bruce about an acquaintance of his who embarked on a short-lived and ill-advised relationship with a younger woman inspired the album's title track. In an interview with John Tobler, McTell noted, 'I've always thought there was an insanity about older blokes trying to get off with a young girl and actually believing for a time that it's all going to work out'. Later, he adds:

> 'Sand in Your Shoes' came to mean all the little memories that I can never lose. The sand in your shoes is either a bit of grit between your toes that irritates you because it's unresolved or something that gives you a pleasant, warm holiday feeling, which I've used as the title of the album. It's non-specific, about refusing to grow up, staying young or accepting your past, as much as offering brotherly advice.

Despite the song's subject matter, there is a lightness of tone to the piece. Playful references to Doctor Watson and Sherlock Holmes and a phoenix rising from the ashes of the affair's inevitable conflagration prepare one for the song's closing sentiment: 'You might grow old, but you won't grow up/If you keep a little sand in your shoes'.

'Jesus Wept' (McTell)

Here, McTell once more turns his attention to matters of faith, this time targeting organised religion. Inspired in part by a television play by Dennis Potter (1935-1994) called *Son Of Man*, it's clearly a song of a non-believer, one that echoes questions many sceptics have asked over the years, and one that makes painfully clear how poorly humans have interpreted and acted on Christ's original teachings. McTell's Jesus is a very human figure, demonstrative, doubtful ('the biggest miracle was that anyone believed it'), fearful ('He wondered would the nails hurt') and even capricious in his doubts about Peter. His last thoughts are of his earthly mother and father. Obviously, then, McTell's feelings for the human Christ are deep. The world would be a better, more compassionate place if his message were followed more often by those who celebrate him as the son of God. If Jesus wept, then McTell is weeping with him.

'After Rain' (McTell)

In 1964, scientists first gave a name to a sensation we have all experienced. They described the scent produced after rainfall as 'petrichor', a term derived by combining the Greek words for stone (*petra*) and *ikhor*, roughly translated as the blood of the gods. Usually optimistic in his view of life, McTell has increasingly come to appreciate the value of looking for silver linings in dark clouds. Here, each stanza includes a concession to the difficulties of life but closes with the reassurance that 'the earth smells sweeter after rain'. The gentle song is another example of McTell's use of water imagery. Besides rain, McTell includes the words 'deluge', 'floods' and 'teardrops' to portray the destructive and redemptive power of this most common and necessary of compounds. Obvious parallels abound with McTell's earlier track, 'Another Rain Has Fallen'.

'Peppers And Tomatoes' (McTell)

Though general enough to be applicable to many civil wars, this powerful song of protest was inspired by the unrest in Yugoslavia in the late 1980s and early 1990s. The story is told by a figure in the neighbourhood minority who is growing more and more wary of contemporary events. The song is constructed expertly. As the man's worries build, verse by verse, the chorus, demonstrating the faith he's placed in his roots, demonstrates ever-diminishing consolation.

> Oh, this little patch of dirt, oh this little pile of stones
> I can wash the dust from off my face and off my skin
> But this earth is in my bones.

Whereas in the first verse, the narrator contrasts himself with his neighbours ('I grow peppers and tomatoes... they grow beans and potatoes'), in the second, he uses the pronoun 'we' and stresses their similarities. A feeling of 'love thy neighbour' prevails for a short time. Soldiers enter the song in the third verse, and in the fourth, the narrator's choice of wine is contrasted by the others' choice of beer. The fifth verse is pivotal. At its conclusion, the narrator feels alienation by the fact that others are singing songs that he doesn't know. In the sixth verse, we learn the source of the tension: religious differences between the two groups. By the seventh verse, the man is preparing to flee, and in the eighth, he states his resolve to fight back, even if it costs him his life. By the final verse, it becomes clear he has left things too late. In the present tense, he describes how he hears the faceless soldiers utter the phrase that has become a terrifying euphemism: 'You must come with us'. The song jerks to a halt powerfully, leaving the listener in little doubt as to the narrator's fate.

'The Case Of Otto Schwarzkopf' (Huppert/McTell/Allcock)

A tragedy set to music, this song is based on a poem by Shmuel Huppert (1936-2006), an Israeli scholar who was imprisoned in Bergen-Belsen during the Second World War. As the track that follows 'Peppers And Tomatoes', it is an eerie reminder of the extremes to which racial cleansing can be taken. While we have Huppert to thank for the ingenious device of centring the piece around an inanimate suitcase (long on exhibit in a museum), we can applaud McTell's arrangement and his taste in bringing the composition to a new audience. Producer Maartin Allcock lends an appropriately haunting piano accompaniment.

'Daddy's Whistling Home' (McTell)
Set to a big band tune that is upbeat enough to sound ironic, this track finds McTell returning to the father theme he has explored previously. The song is more subtle than either of McTell's earlier pieces, however. The listener is being shown, not told, the results of the father's behaviour, an act of infidelity hinted at early in the piece but only confirmed in the third-to-last line. His post-war family is struggling to make ends meet. Typically, for McTell, the mother is portrayed as hard-working and long-suffering. Instead of wishing on a star, she is looking to the heavens for some sort of answer to the question she is afraid to ask her husband: who is the other woman? The image of the supposedly relaxed, whistling father stands in stark contrast to the anxious, listening mother. She blames their lack of lovemaking on her husband's attempts to improve himself, and thus the lot of his family, by taking evening school classes. The image of the mother looking for the stars through the blackout curtains aptly illustrates the futility of her hopes. The truth is veiled yet evident. Though she is able to sing in her kitchen, her ears are more intent on hearing the sound of her husband's whistling. One is left wondering if a confrontation looms or whether the mother will continue to explain away and tolerate her husband's actions in order to at least preserve a façade of domestic harmony for the sake of her children. McTell has noted the irony in the fact that his mother used to fancy the hit song, 'I Wonder Who's Kissing Her Now', from the 1909 musical, *The Prince Of Tonight*.

'Still In Dreams' (McTell)
Easily the prettiest song on the album, 'Still In Dreams' effectively captures the dream-like state of embarking on another day, even when one is ill-prepared to put one's best foot forward. Whether the cause of the narrator's daze is jet lag or a more general recovery from another kind of flight is, in the end, immaterial. Listeners have all experienced the sight of our mirrored faces, 'weathered in time's wilderness'. Lyrically poetic and musically beautiful, this is a track that demands our attention and repeated listening.

'An Irish Blessing' (McTell)
In some ways, 'An Irish Blessing' updates 1979's 'Love Grows'. The children have begun to leave home and McTell, the father, realises that as much as he'd like to tread with them, 'their uncertain road' they must tread alone. He

employs a traditional Irish blessing – in the original and English translation – as the chorus: 'May the road rise with you/And the wind be at your back.' Learning to let go is perhaps the final lesson that parents must learn and it can be a difficult one. Here, McTell, the parent, comes full circle and contrasts the feelings expressed in his earlier songs to those he's now experiencing: 'To cherish is the easy part/The hardest task is letting go'. Though the lyric's appeal is universal, the use of uilleann pipes, fiddle and whistle lend it an appropriately Irish flavour. The final couplet is a worthy benediction and serves as an apt conclusion to the album: 'May my love be your protector/And walk with you till next we meet'.

Red Sky (2000)

Personnel:
Ralph McTell: guitar, vocals
Dave Pegg: bass
Gerry Conway: drums, percussion
Alan Thomson: bass, piano
Chris Parkinson: accordion, melodeon, concertina, harmonica, organ
Steve Turner: guitar, lap steel guitar, dobro
Chris While: backing vocals
Julie Matthews: backing vocals
Mike Piggott: violin
Maartin Allcock: fretless bass, double bass, bouzar, organ, keyboards
Recorded at Woodworm Studios, 2000
Produced by Ralph McTell
UK release date: month, 2000
Highest chart places: did not chart
Running time: 74:03

Featuring 19 selections, not to mention a hidden track, *Red Sky* is McTell's longest album, clocking in at just over 74 minutes. Though leavened by songs like 'Icarus Survived The Fall', 'I Love Driving West' and 'One Day Away From You', the collection is largely dour in tone. Couples fight, grow weary of each other and separate. Indeed, separation is said to be the theme of the album. The world is portrayed as a place that features numerous challenges and pitfalls.

Though McTell includes a song whose narrator claims he isn't really blue, the album's gravitas can seem a bit of a downer at times. Many of the selections are excellent, however, and another way to regard the collection is as an album of realism, one whose protagonists struggle, but are willing to keep giving life a go in hopes that their efforts will eventually pay off. The usual crack team of musicians lend their magic to proceedings, including backing vocalists Chris While and Julie Matthews, who came to prominence with the Albion Band and later recorded multiple projects together. The gothic cover photograph appropriately shows a solitary figure silhouetted against a red sky.

David Kidman, a regular reviewer of McTell's output for NetRhythm, describes the album as 'an undisputed pinnacle of Ralph's achievement'. Though he acknowledges that a few of the tracks are rather bland, he finds here 'more than enough evidence that his considerable powers of observation have not waned one jot and that his voice is still as warm and enticing as ever. He shows himself capable of expressing himself artistically through a wide variety of musical styles with almost equal credibility'. Rob Beattie (*Q Magazine*, January 2001) calls the album 'McTell's best record for 25 years', giving special praise to 'Easter Lilies', 'Bicker And Rue' and 'Fin'.

'Up' (McTell)
The album's opening track revisits a theme developed in earlier McTell songs: one must acknowledge life's challenges before working to overcome them. The freedom/confinement imagery of 'Throw Out A Line' and 'Tous Les Animaux' is once more explored in this thoughtful composition. True bravery exists only when we are fully aware of our fears.

'Wagon On The Motorway' (McTell)
If the previous track celebrated vertical progress, this one is more horizontal in nature and captures a memorable moment in time. The mature narrator is reminded of his past via a glimpse of a youthful driver. McTell's observation that 'freedom's more than just the price of diesel' is poignant, while the song's chorus is a fine summation of the couple's odyssey: 'The road was a ball of string they were unravelling/Looping words to the story they were travelling'.

'In The Dreamtime' (McTell)
McTell toured Australia on numerous occasions and always went over well down under. The concept of the 'dreamtime', life's genesis, is central to Aboriginal beliefs. The 'southern cross' from the lyrics refers to the clusters of stars that represent a possum, the sky deity, Mirrabooka. Distance, both geographical and emotional, is a key theme in the composition. The resulting perspective is often required in order to better understand what lies immediately before us. Both McTell's vocals and the song's production lend a tranquil, soothing quality to the recording. Gerry Conway's percussion work is particularly noteworthy. It is an outstanding piece.

'One Day Away From You' (McTell)
The tone changes entirely in the following track, though separation is once again central. Throughout the song, the narrator upbraids himself for committing various indiscretions against his love and resolves to do better. Just as the narrator of 'I Don't Think About You' takes listeners into his confidence, here they are once more privy to intimacies. In both songs, the narrator has come to grips with who he is and all that this realisation implies. He is weak, he is fallible, he is human. By portraying his narrators as representatives of the common man, McTell thus bridges any gap that may exist between himself as an artist and his audience. The track's country feel and McTell's vocals are similarly inviting. Steve Turner's guitar work is worthy of a Nashville session.

'Lost Boys' (McTell)
A raucous tune driven by Mike Piggott's insistent fiddle, 'Lost Boys' is McTell's take on J.M. Barrie's Neverland lads who find savour in life by taking chances. The composer's admiration for them is evident.

'Bicker And Rue' (McTell)

Told by an omniscient narrator who assigns no blame to either partner, this song moves along at a good pace and adheres strictly to an established form. The first verse plays off of the old notion of the spouse as ball and chain. McTell thus immediately conjures a tension between the man and woman on display. In the ensuing verses, he deftly catalogues the reasons behind their verbal melee. Wonderfully contrasting details emerge in verse after verse ('The warp and the weft both parts of the weave/The rough tweed jacket with a silk-lined sleeve') as the piece tensely builds towards a climax. One senses the bedtime truce (reminiscent of 'Summer Lightning') that is reached by the song's end is only temporary. If the lovers sometimes feel chained together like prisoners, they also realise these ties will never come unbound. Ultimately, they will, in fact, win the three-legged race that is domestic life. McTell's earlier portrayal of Dylan Thomas and his wife, Caitlin, may have helped him here.

'Now This Has Started' (McTell)

This atmospheric track details the thunderous effect 'a certain look, a certain smile' from another can impart. One feels McTell is addressing himself along with his listeners. No doubt he, too, is not immune to the sort of temptation that makes peace of mind impossible. How sinister such feelings can become is revealed in the third verse where 'love' as possession echoes a theme explored in 'Tous Les Animaux Sont Tristes'. McTell was inspired to write the song by the scene in *The Godfather* where Michael Corleone falls in love at first sight with Apollonia while exiled in Sicily. In *Summer Lightning* (88), he elaborates on the feeling:

> The pain of longing for someone is never so intense as when you are young; the effect that this state has on you makes your whole body and mind behave oddly. The intensity of feeling, the appropriateness of every silly love song to your situation and the deep dark knowledge that the object of your affection and the causer of your pain isn't even aware of your existence, let alone your name.

That McTell should write this song as a middle-aged man serves to emphasise the intensity of love, no matter at what age it happens to overwhelm us.

'Easter Lilies' (McTell)

'Easter Lilies' is a fascinating and complex song which McTell has often been asked about. His intention was to keep the lyrics ambiguous in order to lend it an air of mystery. While some listeners have wondered if it concerns suicide, McTell intended it to suggest triumph, a new beginning (as the title suggests), optimism and, ultimately, survival. Easter lilies in Norway are what the English call daffodils. Schweigaardsgate is in Oslo, and in fact, the story was based on his Norwegian sister-in-law, Astrid. McTell, in a 20 May 2003 interview with the author:

> The daffodil sort of trumpets the shape of their little flowers and sort of trumpets a new beginning, if you like. The idea of her filling her room with flowers to symbolise a new beginning and creating this atmosphere – it sounds like she's preparing herself for a sort of self-sacrifice, bathing, cleansing, and that's the suspense in the song. It's just about how things really can turn like that.

'Raining In My Heart' (Bryant/Bryant)
An interesting inclusion on an album that features so many original songs, this standard, written by hit-makers Felice and Boudleaux Bryant, is pleasant if not particularly memorable.

'Icarus Survived The Fall' (McTell)
In this optimistic take on the story from Greek mythology, McTell transforms one of the most recognisable representatives of human folly into a kind of hero. He gives Icarus his turn to speak and his advice is considerable. If not leavened by humour, however, his pronouncements, and the entire song would flop as badly as his original flight. Again, the mature McTell recognises that an entirely earnest statement of this sort would not succeed. Attitude is everything.

'Saucers (Aquamarine)' (McTell)
'Saucers' was the nickname McTell's father gave to McTell's mother due to her large, pale blue eyes. Contrasting with the 'steel imbedded in her soul' is the image of her husband as 'the blade that missed her heart'. Whence she came by the steel to withstand such an assault is a mystery to her admiring son. Water imagery (always a favourite of McTell's) runs throughout the entire song. His mother's aquamarine eyes are 'The colour of spring water' and 'at the shoreline's edge', they are 'of a lighter hue' than the water 'hidden in deeper blue'. Water, the most common liquid on earth, is also, like mothers, the giver of all life. Some of McTell's most mature poetry lies in the song. The last verse, in particular, is noteworthy. The image of his mother's 'calloused, chapped' hands 'inside a velvet glove' hiding 'the scars and grip of love' beautifully restates the notion that 'beauty is skin deep'. Though in his autobiographical writings, he discloses that his mother was rarely affectionate towards him and his brother, his admiration for her other qualities is abundant in this touching song.

'When Love Has Gone' (McTell)
Here, as in so many other McTell compositions, the perseverance of love is celebrated. Numerous riddles dot the song, and a number of different

perspectives are employed by the composer. In a 30 May 2004 email to the author, McTell explained that the song can apply to many kinds of love, including that experienced by siblings. If some details remain elusive, the piece reminds us that even though it may seem so at heated moments of separation ('reason's anger's casualty'), love never completely vanishes. Even when difficulties obscure feelings once treasured, memories of better times remain.

'Let Me Fly Or Let Me Fall' (McTell)

As the title implies, this is a song of opposites and dichotomies. Whether or not it depicts a sexual relationship is open to interpretation, but here again, separation is a theme. The first three verses use a common structure that contrasts the roles the narrator and his addressed companion have played in what appears to be a lengthy relationship. In the first verse, McTell returns to imagery he has employed previously, that of the martyr ('Jesus Wept') and the entertainer ('Clown'). Under the influence of his companion, the narrator claims to have been transformed into both. McTell defines the spectrum this creates with the epigrammatic line: 'The difference between church and stage/Is whether we're enlightened or amazed'. The second verse picks up the theme by contrasting thinking and laughter, and then flying and falling. That either flying or falling can be effective or positive is demonstrated by the line: 'It (letting one fall) can sometimes fire the engines when they stall' (In fact, the song was suggested to McTell by hearing a story of a pilot who 'bump started' a jet whose engines had stalled). To exist in an uncommitted state ('to float without the drive') is no way to live. The sum of the relationship must equal more than 'being half alive'. Only in the third verse is a past ('I used to turn you on') or present ('Ah, but love has never gone') sexual relationship suggested. Yet as quickly as love is intimated, the narrator acknowledges that there exists between them 'a weakening of something strong'. The fourth verse abandons the previous structure of 'used to'. It is time to move on now, time to 'take some chances' if they hope to progress in any meaningful way. The use of the driving metaphor effectively defines this need and neatly closes the song. To live safely, to deny another his freedom to fly or fall, is not to live life to its fullest. Though the lyric is complex, the musicians achieved the recording in a single take.

'I Suppose' (McTell)

A rocking track by McTell's standards, 'I Suppose' is a song of reflection and regret that employs parallel constructions. Numerous images of violence included here are atypical of McTell's work.

'I Love Driving West' (McTell)

This song picks up the driving/travel theme first explored in 'Wagon On The Motorway' and, unlike many other tracks on the album, is quite straightforward.

'I'm Not Really Blue' (McTell)
McTell admits to trying to outdo the McGarrigle Sisters' classic song, 'Heart Like A Wheel' on this selection, a meditation on coping and moving on.

'Fin' (McTell)
'Fin' celebrates Nanna May's love for French noir films popular when the couple were courting in Paris in the 1960s. McTell succeeds here both in poking fun at some of the head-scratching conventions of such movies and expressing a genuine admiration for them and the larger-than-life figures who brought them to life on the big screen.

'I'll Keep This With Mine (Leaving 'Liggan Woods)' (McTell)
Yet another song of separation, whose title was perhaps inspired by Dylan's 'I'll Keep it With Mine', this track was based on a couple known to McTell who lived a rugged, rural existence. The melody came to him upon awakening one morning, one of only two instances in which this occurred. McTell's vocals are muted in tribute to the sorrow he feels. Steve Turner's plaintive, haunting guitar adds to the pathos inherent in the piece.

'Red Sky At Night' (McTell)
A slow, mournful tune that also features a rural setting, the song from which the album takes its title is the sad tale of a farmer losing his land. The blow is apparently unexpected, as McTell alters the famous nautical weather rhyme to state, 'there will not be any warning/There's going to be a red sky tonight'. The piece is performed solo, thereby mimicking the shepherd's solitary steps and isolation. The song ends after about four minutes and 20 seconds but then resumes again via a two-minute hidden track that commences nine minutes in. The fact that this is a jaunty ragtime guitar piece seems to indicate that McTell hopes to dispel some of the gloom that has pervaded the entire album.

Somewhere Down The Road (2010)

Personnel:
Ralph McTell: guitar, harmonica, bouzouki, drums, vocals
Tim Renwick: guitar
Willie Wilson: drums
Dave Quinn: bass
Chris Parkinson: accordion, pan pipes
James Hallawell: piano
Steve Turner: double bass, guitar
John Dowling: banjo
John Cornfield: percussion
Christy Shearcroft: backing vocals
Anna Dowling: backing vocals
Veronica Woodburn: violin
Karen Frost: violin
Chris Prindl: viola
Barbara Degener: cello
Recorded at Woodlane Studios, April-July 2010
Produced by John Cornfield
UK release date: 2010
Highest chart places: did not chart
Running time: 64:02

Released ten years after its predecessor, *Somewhere Down The Road* is a solid collection of songs, ably produced by John Cornfield who, here, favours sparse arrangements. McTell returns to his blues roots in two selections and two distinct themes emerge in the other 12 tracks. If the pull of the past is on full display in 'Moon June', 'Girl On The Jersey Ferry', 'Lantern Slides' and 'A Kiss In The Rain', the learning process is central to four other pieces. 'The London Apprentice' learns that 'a man who never makes any mistakes never makes anything at all'; the narrator of 'Walk Into The Morning' learns the lessons of the road; a young man sailing round Cape Horn learns that 'if you want to love your life you have to flirt with death'; and self-centred 'Rosalinda' learns that 'as long as there is light there won't be endless night'. Old friend Peter Thaine, who had designed the covers of *Spiral Staircase* and *My Side Of Your Window,* here depicts a greying McTell heading off to his next gig with a look of determined resolve.

David Kidman's lengthy, insightful review of the album for NetRhythms is enthusiastic. He notes that 'the spirit of place informs and inspires deeper philosophical reflections', and also highlights how 'The passage of time in the context of life's journey inevitably figures large'. Kidman admires the 'array of musical influences and idioms' included while pointing out that 'such flavours are always kept at the service of the song and never gratuitously applied'. The reviewer concludes that 'All in all, *Somewhere Down The Road* is magnificent and a real triumph, not least in that it serves to unify the strands of Ralph's musical and philosophical psyche in a thoroughly convincing, both thought-provoking and entertaining way'.

'The London Apprentice' (McTell)
A tribute to his beloved capital city, the opening track is a mature meditation on the fact that we all make mistakes, never fully master life and must continually be prepared to make new beginnings. Chris Parkinson's accordion drives the tightly structured recording.

'Reverend Thunder (Blind Faith)' (McTell)
Based largely on the grit and tenacity of one of McTell's musical heroes, the Reverend Gary Davis (1896-1972), this song is an apt depiction of the saying that the Lord helps those who help, or in this case, defend themselves. McTell sounds happy to be returning to his blues roots here and allows his guitar fills to take the place of lyrics in observance of the tradition.

'Walk Into The Morning' (McTell)
A stroll down memory lane for McTell and another homage to apprenticeship, 'Walk into the Morning' recounts the challenges and joys of his early days on the open road. If some of his knowledge is hard-won, it is also instinctive or the result of the examples of others, like Woody Guthrie and Sonny Terry. On a live performance, McTell notes that he did once jam with Sonny Terry and his partner, Brownie McGhee. Though a gentle song, it is positive in tone, a recognition that one must keep moving and learning in order to progress from morning to life's afternoons and evenings. The dust mentioned in the lyric hints at life's impermanence.

'Around The Wild Cape Horn' (McTell)
A third song of youth gaining valuable experience, 'Around The Wild Cape Horn' is a ballad that adopts a device often employed by Bob Dylan, namely ending each verse with the same line. Occasional changes in tempo and melody keep the long track from becoming monotonous. An indication of the youth's growing maturity is reflected by his adoption of the first-person plural rather than the singular once he has joined the boat's crew.

'The Ghost Of Robert Johnson' (McTell)
Everyone who has tried to play the blues after 1938 betrays the influence of Robert Johnson. Here, McTell includes several references to the doomed singer's work in the form of a hellhound, crossroads and the phrases, 'love in vain' and 'possession over judgement day'. McTell's line, 'eternity lies waiting where imagination and reality collide', is rather profound and picks up the theme of maturation already established in the album's earlier songs. Artists are inherently restless and must keep growing in order to survive. If Johnson

himself was unable to tame his demons, the example he set is quite pervasive in this homage.

'Rosalinda' (McTell)

The Western swing feel of 'Rosalinda' amplifies the encouraging tone of its lyrics. We must rise to life's challenges, not hide from them in self-pity. There are some echoes of Dylan's 'To Ramona' (a favourite of McTell's) in this spirited track filled with advice. McTell artistically begins and ends the composition with window imagery.

'The Break Of The Union' (McTell)

While McTell is sympathetic to Scottish calls for independence, he feels the United Kingdom would lose a great deal if their neighbours to the North were to break away. Here, he acknowledges the brave service Highlanders have performed for years in the British army and compares the union to a marriage of convenience, 'whose dowry's still unpaid'. If the narrator begins with a heavy heart, the listener feels encouraged by the song's end that a possible rupture need not be permanent. The melody recalls the traditional 'The Parting Glass', while the pipe and whistle lend an appropriately Celtic feel.

'Cannabis Creek' (McTell)

In Grenfell's book on McTell (54-55), the composer is quoted as saying that 'Cannabis Creek' 'exaggerates the attraction of opposites as in the way sexual desire overrules racial prejudice'. It is a complex and unusual song that details the potential destructiveness of sexual attraction, a theme also explored in 'Now This Has Started'. The active hippies are contrasted with their observer, whose voyeurism suggests inertia and sterility. McTell based the piece on a small commune on the Fowey River where friends and bandmates Clive Palmer and Whistling Mick Bennett lived for a time in the 1960s. It remains unclear (at least to this listener) if the line, 'a man seems to be destined to destroy the things he loves', suggests that the voyeur called for the destruction of the camp due to his inability to join in the revelry or simply because the object of his lust has disappeared.

'One Sunny Day (Aujourd'hui Le Ciel Est Bleu)' (McTell)

Maite Bell translated McTell's text into French for this song about a call to life after winter's dreariness. A litany of nature imagery supplements the theme.

'Moon June And A Cajun Tune' (McTell)

This lively and enjoyable composition pokes fun at songwriting conventions and hackneyed rhymes just as John Prine did in 'Big Old Goofy World'. Its bridge nicely turns the song in a new direction as the narrator's mind is cast into the past. The listener's takeaway here is that we must not allow the past to ruin the present.

'A Kiss In The Rain' (McTell)
One sign of a mature songwriter is a growing interest in the lives of others rather than a preoccupation with himself. Here, McTell provides a glimpse into the past via the relationship of friends and fellow musicians Annie (Briggs) and Bert (Jansch). Freedom is the dominant theme of this song, which also includes images of the moon and water. The melody recalls Donovan's 'Epistle To Derroll'.

'The Girl On The Jersey Ferry' (McTell)
The track that follows similarly highlights the pull of the past. An ode to romanticism, the song was inspired by a scene from Orson Welles' famous film *Citizen Kane*. Set to a lovely melody and augmented by a charming string arrangement, the composition is an apt example of McTell's philosophy that, in Grenfell's words, 'an instant can open out into an entire world or lifetime'.

'Lantern Slides' (McTell)
'Lantern Slides' stems from a memory associated with McTell's mother, the 'Win' mentioned in the opening line. This is a deeply personal song, but one feels the composer has earned the right to indulge himself. The insertion of the children's choir singing 'Jesus Bids Us Shine' is another indication of McTell's yearning for a past where faith is able to play a supportive role. The introduction of McTell's mother to his father lends the song's conclusion an ominous, almost existential feel.

'Somewhere Down The Road' (McTell)
Perhaps inspired by a line from the last verse of Dylan's 'Song To Woody', this straightforward piece concerns time and the futility of farewells. True friends need never part if their presence can remain as constant as a song both have known and loved. In some ways, the piece hints at eternity or at least what humans attempt to understand by the phrase. If we cannot cheat eternity, we nevertheless try to maximise what time is granted to us. The importance of what former US President Barack Obama dubbed 'the audacity of hope', is also touched on in the piece. The final verse echoes sentiments expressed in another Dylan song, 'Death Is Not The End'.

Hill Of Beans (2019)

Personnel:
Ralph McTell: guitar, piano, vocals
Tony Visconti: recorder, bass, backing vocals
Chris Parkinson: accordion, Hammond organ
Danny Thompson: double bass
Gerry Conway: percussion
Frank Gallagher: mandolin
Dan Block: clarinet
Everton Nelson: violin
Ian Humphries: violin
Bruce White: viola
Emma Owens: viola
Ian Burdge: cello
Chris Worsey: cello
Jessica Morgan: backing vocals
Mary Hopkin: backing vocals
Recorded at Visconti Studios, 2019
Produced by Tony Visconti
UK release date: 2019
Highest chart places: did not chart
Running time: 40:59

Whether this 2019 collection will be McTell's final album of original songs remains to be seen. It is certainly a strong effort, full of life lessons and avuncular advice. If a few of the tracks are overly personal or perhaps a bit obscure, asking too much of the listener, the majority are true to life and moving. Nearly every selection is rooted in the past, but McTell is clearly not mired there. His rich harvest of memories is a gift both to longtime fans and new listeners. McTell turned to Tony Visconti to produce the album, the first time he had enlisted his help in this capacity since 1974. Visconti's deft approach to string arrangements is evident throughout the collection. The black and white cover photo by Chris Lopez shows McTell staring straight into the camera, emanating determination and evincing hard-won experience.

In his review for *Living Tradition*, Dai Woosnam lauds both Visconti's production and the quality of the album's songs, singling out 'Brighton Belle' and 'Close Shave'. Woosnam cites 'West Fourth Street And Jones' as the collection's best song, characterising it as a 'veritable Proustian madeleine cake'.

'Oxbow Lakes' (McTell)

The opening track to McTell's most recent album hearkens back in some ways to 'Throw Out A Line And Dream' in that two distinct approaches to life are explored via a relationship that seems destined to end unhappily. The image of an oxbow lake – cut off from the mainstream flow and now separate – is an apt metaphor and continues McTell's fascination with water imagery. The track has a pleasant country feel, augmented by producer Tony Visconti's recorder.

'Brighton Belle' (McTell)
Similar in some ways to 'Lantern Slides' from the previous album in that it also stems directly from the composer's past, here McTell employs the image of a famous railway engine to trace both historical and personal developments. His paternal grandfather, Charles May, was a railroad engineer who began work in the steam age driving engines that included the one that gives this song its title. He was later quite happy to conclude his career driving diesels, a much cleaner alternative. The war and post-war years are both portrayed, while toil and duty are contrasted with the luxury and leisure that the titular engine embodied. McTell's vocals are confident and conversational in this largely unadorned track.

'Clear Water' (McTell)
A lovely, stately song that features a lush string arrangement and prominent backing vocals. The experienced narrator expresses a longing for clarity via a series of nautical metaphors. It is clear to the listener, however, that resolution is not equated with any kind of simple conclusion. The narrator does not want the journey to be over just yet.

'Gertrude And Alice' (McTell)
McTell's appreciation of the arts and knowledge of France unite in this portrait of Gertrude Stein (1874-1946) and her companion, Alice B. Toklas (1877-1967). McTell tells their story by supplementing snippets from daily life with allusions to the famous members of their circle. The composer's delight in wordplay is apparent throughout. Gertrude finds 'Hemingway paradoxically earnest and frail', for example, and numerous internal rhymes (Alice-Paris, George-forge, look-book to name a few) are included. The rambling and, at times, abstract feel of the piece faithfully reflects the sometimes-obtuse work of Stein and artists like Picasso and Matisse, both mentioned in the piece. Chris Parkinson again provides atmospheric accordion to place the song squarely in Paris.

'Gammel Dansk' (McTell)
For the uninitiated, Gammel Dansk is an alcoholic drink produced in Norway that originated in Denmark. A rough translation of the name is 'old Danish'. McTell was inspired to write the song based on his memories of downtime while on tour in the Scandinavian country. Regarding its particulars, McTell (via an interview on his website) has stated: 'I used the Chagall influence with respect to the seagulls that have become the souls of the dead flying through the bones of events they have witnessed. And this guy is going to fade into

the black and white monochrome world and they won't even find him and they won't find her'. A song with themes of disconnection and impersonality, it is complex and those who have not read the explanation might find its meaning elusive. The Klezmer sound that accompanies the track is quite unusual for a McTell recording.

'Shed Song' (McTell)
This composition uses religious imagery (temple, church, priestly, voodoo, communion) to describe a refuge where a young boy and his grandfather find sanctuary. Though the song ends with the inevitable decay of the shed, it remains a benediction of sorts for childhood memories that far outlast the wooden structure. Though the song is not strictly autobiographical, McTell was similarly fascinated with the shed belonging to his Uncle Reg, an important figure to the fatherless child, and time spent in such temples of masculinity left a deep impression. Strings dominate the accompaniment.

'Close Shave' (McTell)
McTell changes the feel of the album by inserting this ragtime story of suspicion and escape. By the song's end, the listener both suspects the barber's surmise has been correct and is certain that McTell has greatly enjoyed revisiting the music of his youth.

'When They Were Young' (McTell)
An openly sentimental song leavened by McTell's matter-of-fact delivery, 'When They Were Young' is a reflection on the nature of love that goes beyond lust. The composer's use of tree imagery is inventive and the acknowledgement that love can be just as restrictive as it is liberating is instructive.

'Sometimes I Wish I Could Pray' (McTell)
Though previously released as a bonus track on the CD release of *Slide Away The Screen*, here McTell grants the song a much larger feel, including the vital addition of backing vocals that evoke a church choir. Non-believers can certainly relate to McTell's stated desire to 'believe that everything has been planned in advance' by a benevolent God. In the second volume of his autobiography, *Summer Lightning* (220), McTell describes observing a congregation at mass in Florence where he felt 'a pang of envy at their corporate act of worship and belonging to something'. The boy who looked for Mrs Adlam's angels is still open to the possibility of the divine here.

'Hill Of Beans' (McTell, and title phrase under copyright control)
Just as he had evoked a scene from *Citizen Kane* on his previous album, here, McTell recounts the sacrifice made by Rick in an equally famous film, *Casablanca*.

'West 4th Street And Jones' (McTell)

McTell saves the best for last. If he had treated a famous film scene in the proceeding track, here McTell tells the story of a famous image, the cover photo from one of his favourite albums – the groundbreaking 1963 album, *The Freewheelin' Bob Dylan*. McTell nicely captures Dylan's studied nonchalance and gift for making the affected seem genuine. Like Rick and Ilsa in *Casablanca*, Dylan and his girlfriend, Suze Rotolo, would eventually part ways, but in this frozen moment in time, they are united in youthful love. Lovers drift apart, but art and memory eternally unite them. In the penultimate verse, McTell compares his own doomed love affair to the more famous couple's, linking his life to Dylan's. The famed Nobel Prize winner later heard the song and wrote McTell a note, stating that 'it made an old man cry'. Though he never came close to matching Dylan's success, mass appeal or influence, Ralph McTell has left a memorable legacy of his own, both eternally and for tomorrow.

Cover Albums

Though they pale in importance to his collection of original material, the seven cover albums discussed below represent a major part of the second half of Ralph McTell's career. While he released 11 albums of original material between 1968 and 1987, the 32 years since have seen him produce only five. During that period, McTell covered more than 80 songs written by his main influences: country blues performers as well as Woody Guthrie and Bob Dylan. Though the subject of this book eventually took a stage name from Blind Willie McTell, he was also nicknamed Woody early in his career due to his affection for the Dust Bowl Balladeer. Guthrie inspired McTell to explore the world by taking to the road. He also instilled in the young man left-wing politics that extolled a working man's value and, perhaps most importantly, lent proof to a notion that one didn't have to be a great musician to be a powerful songwriter. For his part, Dylan updated Guthrie, liberated an entire generation of writers by discarding the old 'rule book' and added a 'street attitude' that McTell and untold thousands of others found irresistible.

Any performer who covers another artist's work is aware of the risks involved and must consider certain questions. Will they be regarded as mere imitators? Might their fans fear they are resorting to covers due to a creative dry spell? Do they have anything significantly new to bring to the original recording? While interpretations such as Jimi Hendrix's transformation of Bob Dylan's 'All Along the Watchtower', Elvis Presley's vision for Big Mama Thornton's 'Hound Dog' or Joe Cocker's new spin on The Beatles' 'A Little Help From My Friends' are rare, they do indicate the potential of covers. At such moments, an entirely different piece of art can be created. Few of McTell's covers described below are transformative in this manner. They are intended as homages to the songwriters he most admired and succeed admirably in this respect.

At The End Of A Perfect Day (1985)

Personnel:
Ralph McTell: guitar, vocals
Linda Allan: backing vocals
Jerry Conway: drums and percussion
Nick Curtis: backing vocals
Stephanie de Sykes: backing vocals
Jerry Donahue: guitar
Howard Evans: trumpet
Jimmy Leverton: bass, guitar
Leah May: backing vocals
Jerry Shirley: drums and percussion
Roger Williams: trombone
Alun Davies: guitar
Produced by Graham Preskett and Ralph McTell
UK release date: 1985
Highest chart places: did not chart
Running time: 52:33

A low ebb in McTell's career, this album largely consists of selections that were hits for other singer-songwriters. The very title is a confusing choice since Chris de Burgh had used the same phrase for his 1977 release. McTell's heart was never in the project, as his listless performances indicate. If the tracks aren't truly poor, they lack any real spark. Performers need a good reason to record another writer's material other than to try to please would-be listeners, expand their audience or because they are short on new original compositions themselves. McTell had always feared the label of MOR performer, and, with few exceptions, that is how even his most loyal fans must classify these tracks. Subtitled '16 Songs Of Love And Friendship', the album also features a few re-recordings of McTell originals. The cover is as bland as its material, depicting a fresh-scrubbed McTell walking down an avenue at dusk. Even the look on his face looks manufactured for the occasion.

'Streets Of London' (McTell)
The fact that the album opens with McTell trotting out his hit is an immediate sign of desperation.

'Scarborough Fair' (Trad.)
Well-intentioned but cheesy backing vocals doom this cover of Simon and Garfunkel's arrangement of the classic English folk song.

'You've Got A Friend' (King)
A standard reading of the Carole King composition popularised by James Taylor.

'Penny Lane' (Lennon-McCartney)
There's a certain forced cheeriness to this cover of The Beatles' classic. When McTell sings 'very strange' just before each chorus, he could be summarising the thought process behind the entire album.

'The Lamplighter' (McTell)
The performance of this McTell classic shows little variation from the original found on *Spiral Staircase*.

'The Last Farewell' (Whitaker/Webster)
A perfectly fine cover of Roger Whitaker's famous composition.

'Sailing' (Sutherland)
Rod Stewart scored a huge hit with this Sutherland Brothers song. Poorly chosen synthesiser fills tarnish McTell's cover.

'Beautiful Dreamer' (Foster)
McTell's gentle voice is a good fit for this Stephen Foster classic, but the performer lends little emotion to the reading.

'Homeward Bound' (Simon)
Another performance that fails to find a style of its own.

'Scarlet Ribbons' (Segal/Danzig)
The nature of this song must have appealed to McTell, the father of four, but the track again sounds a bit antiseptic.

'I'll Have To Say I Love You In A Song' (Croce)
Like McTell, Jim Croce balanced his nice-guy persona with compositions that often had a certain edge. This cover of the 1974 posthumous hit never really finds its wings.

'Morning Has Broken' (Trad.)
A saccharine choir dominates this performance of the traditional song that Cat Stevens lent a certain magic to in his 1971 cover. Again, McTell's vocals simply sound safe.

'Weather The Storm' (McTell)
Another very good McTell composition that here sounds a bit rushed compared to the 1976 original.

'Those Were The Days' (Raskin)
Mary Hopkin had a hit with this interesting song in 1969 and perhaps McTell's handlers felt lightning might strike twice. Again, the performance is

flat and the feel of the backing vocals is not suited to the wistful nature of the lyrics.

'Barges' (McTell)
Nearly identical to the original found on 1972's *Not Till Tomorrow*.

'England' (McTell)
Three years previous to this release, McTell included this strong composition on his *Water Of Dreams* album. He puts in a strong shift here if, again, the results do not differ greatly from the original.

Blue Skies Black Heroes (1988)

Personnel:
Ralph McTell: guitar, Dobro, vocals, harmonica
Danny Thompson: double bass
Recorded at Raezor Studio
Produced by Ralph McTell
UK release date: 1988
Running time: 52:12

At some point in their career, nearly every performer returns to their roots, the songs that first motivated them to pick up an instrument in order to attempt to emulate their early heroes. In the album's liner notes, McTell describes the appeal of the blues: 'The dazzling guitar techniques, the simple, uncluttered poetry, the humour and allusion and the whole range of expression contained and controlled in their work are the criteria that I aspire to in my own music'. While McTell had included covers of country blues standards in his earliest albums, here he devotes an entire collection to the songs he cut his musical teeth on. If they are not what distinguish McTell or make him an important artist, these tracks are generally well executed and enjoyable and should best be heard as examples of cultural appreciation, not appropriation. There is more grace than grit to them. The songs were recorded live. The album was the first McTell recording to be released on CD. The unusual cover painting, 'Out Of The Blue', is by Peter Griffin.

'Truckin' Lil' Babe' (Blind Boy Fuller)
Since McTell often used to open his sets with this fun, upbeat Blind Boy Fuller number, it's an appropriate choice to begin the proceedings. Fuller's song was called 'Truckin' My Blues Away' and is much slower in tempo than McTell's interpretation. McTell is playing a Dobro on this track.

'Coalman Blues' (Howell)
McTell again ups the tempo on this Peg Leg Howell tune that is quite macabre in places.

'Fables Ain't Nothing But Doggone Lies' (Jesse Fuller)
The lyrics to this Jesse Fuller song are much more complex and interesting than most blues numbers. How many blues compositions mention Aesop's fables, for example? The lesson we learn is that no matter how you try to spin something, it is still simply a falsehood.

'Drybone Shuffle' (Blake)
Arthur Blake is one of McTell's musical heroes. It's clear to any listener that McTell has performed this upbeat ragtime instrumental hundreds of times. Before he honed his craft as a songwriter, McTell made a living performing

pieces like this one to appreciative audiences. Percussive bones augmented Blake's original recording but are omitted here.

'Louis Collins' (Hurt)
A lovely, stately dirge composed by Mississippi John Hurt, the subject of great admiration for many a guitarist, including Tom Paxton, whose 'Did You Hear John Hurt' expressed what many felt when the bluesman was coaxed out of retirement in the 1960s. McTell sticks close to Hurt's original recording.

'Love In Vain' (Johnson)
If many musicians admired Hurt, even more worshipped at the shrine of the influential Robert Johnson. Here, McTell is faithful to Johnson's original.

'Can't Be Satisfied' (Morganfield, aka Muddy Waters)
McTell's Dobro stylings lift his cover of this Muddy Waters classic.

'Corinne What Makes You Treat Me So Bad' (Blind Boy Fuller)
This track features one of McTell's best vocal performances on the album. His natural baritone warmth perfectly captures the anguish felt by the narrator.

'Statesboro Blues' (Blind Willie McTell)
Even though he took his stage name from the composer of this song, Ralph McTell doesn't include as many of his namesake's tunes in his repertoire compared to some of his other heroes. In *Summer Lightning* (206), McTell writes, 'the impact of this track was as great as Jack Elliott's 'San Francisco Bay Blues' had been. The clear, beautiful voice and intriguing lyric pulled me deeper into the tune, but above all, it was the sound of the 12-string guitar'. Bob Dylan wrote a wonderful song in Blind Willie McTell's honour, while the Allman Brothers' electric version of 'Statesboro Blues' has become a standard.

'Arthur Blake' (Ralph McTell)
Here, McTell communicates as much as any of us know about the mysterious and talented Arthur Blake. The tribute is a welcome addition to the album and showcases McTell's considerable picking skills.

'Kindhearted Woman' (Johnson)
McTell revisits this Robert Johnson tune, first covered on his *Spiral Staircase* album. This listener prefers that version due to the inclusion of a tasty harmonica solo.

'Untrue Blues' (Blind Boy Fuller)
As if in reply to Johnson's homage to a good woman, here McTell performs one of the many blues tales of a cruel woman who just won't treat her man the way she should.

'Early This Morning' (Blake)
Though perhaps better known for his upbeat rags, Blind Blake also sang a good many songs, such as this one, that have a more traditional blues feel.

'Working On The Railroad' (Jesse Fuller)
Fuller's original was called 'Railroad Worksong'. The track has been covered by many besides McTell, including the Notting Hillbillies, a one-shot group led by Mark Knopfler.

'Leah's Favourite' (Ralph McTell)
McTell named this original instrumental after his daughter when she expressed a particular affection for it as he practised the piece at home. Though pleasant, the track has a different sort of feel to it than the album's other selections, sounding more like a number better suited for another project.

'I Bid You Goodnight' (Spence)
On his tribute to Joseph Spence, 'Hands Of Joseph', McTell included portions of this melody. It is, of course, a fitting valedictory to this charming album.

Stealin' Back (1990)

Personnel:
Ralph McTell: guitar, vocals, harmonica, banjo, accordion, Dobro
Mike Piggott: mandolin, violin
Keith Nichols: piano
Graham Read: sousaphone
Roger Williams: trombone
Mick Bennett: backing vocals
Graham Preskett: piano
Recorded at Raezor Studios, July-September 1990.
Produced by Ralph McTell
UK release date: 1990
Running time: 52:50

Stealin' Back is quite similar to *Blue Skies Black Heroes* both in material and approach, though here, there is a heavier emphasis on jug-band music. The black-and-white cover photo by Mike Smallcombe shows McTell cradling his acoustic guitar. Reviewing the album for *Q Magazine*, John Bauldie prefers McTell's ragtime guitar skills to his attempts to sing the blues. He concludes by writing that 'As an exercise in repaying dues, though – and perhaps in exorcising a few ghosts and guilts – it's not without its merits'.

'I'm Going To Germany' (Cannon)
This is a beautifully executed track that showcases McTell's ability as an interpreter. He gradually folds in banjo and accordion to lend texture to the song, originally recorded by Gus Cannon. The destination of Germany in the title refers not to the European country but rather to the red-light district where the narrator hopes to gain some consolation.

'Sugar Babe' (Lipscombe)
McTell's guitar work on this Mance Lipscombe tune is inventive.

'Prison Wall Blues' (Cannon)
As he often does on his blues covers, McTell ups the tempo on the second Gus Cannon piece included on the album.

'Hesitation Blues' (Trad.)
Based on the Reverend Gary Davis' recording, this traditional song does not differ greatly from the version included on McTell's debut album.

'Weeping Willow' (Fuller)
McTell's mentor, Wizz Jones, introduced him to this haunting Blind Boy Fuller tune. The fact that the song's lyrics are more poetic than most blues numbers undoubtedly appealed to McTell.

'When You Got A Good Friend' (Johnson)
McTell's sensitive reading of this Robert Johnson song acutely captures the sense of regret that pervades it and his harmonica work is wonderfully expressive.

'Candy Man' (Trad.)
Another standard covered by hundreds of interpreters, perhaps most famously by Mississippi John Hurt. The soft backing vocals McTell includes provide a new element to this performance.

'When Did You Leave Heaven?' (Whiting/Bullock)
This lovely composition was originally included in the 1936 film *Sing, Sing, Sing*. While not strictly a blues number, many performers, including McTell, came to it via Big Bill Broonzy's version. Bob Dylan covered the song on his *Down In The Groove* album. Mike Piggott's sensitive violin distinguishes McTell's interpretation.

'Stealin'' (Trad.)
McTell is in full jug band mode on the album's title track. His prominent harmonica work is nicely augmented by Graham Read's sousaphone, Roger Williams' trombone and Piggott's mandolin. Old pal Mick Bennett lends vocal support as well. For any interested listeners, Arlo Guthrie's version of 'Stealin'' is quite outstanding.

'That'll Do Babe' (McTell)
McTell titled this catchy, original guitar instrumental after Oliver Hardy, whose nickname was Babe. Though a large man, Hardy was apparently a wonderful dancer. The listener thus gains a nice mental image of Hardy's footwork, as illustrated by the guitar. It has become a staple in McTell's live performances.

'Black Girl' (Trad.)
McTell learnt this song from a Lead Belly recording. Often called 'In The Pines' or 'Where Did You Sleep Last Night', its lyrics are haunting, even sinister. McTell's harmonica nicely captures the ominous feel of the tune.

'Sweet Petulie' (Blake)
McTell plays this down-tempo Blind Blake song (called 'Tootie Blues' on the original recording) on his Dobro. The tricky tempo changes are typical of Blake's work and McTell handles them well here.

'Nobody Knows When You're Down And Out' (Cox)
Eric Clapton's supergroup, Derek And The Dominoes, lent this Jimmie Cox composition a high profile when they included it on their landmark 1970 album, *Layla And Other Assorted Love Songs*. Clapton also included an acoustic version on his *Unplugged* album, released two years after McTell's

version heard here. Bessie Smith's excellent interpretation is also well known. Roger Williams' trombone solo recalls the jazzy spirit of the song's original 1923 composition date.

'Lovin' I Crave' (Blake)
McTell can't get enough of Blind Blake. Here, he plays the tune on his 1934 Gibson L1. McTell's interpretation is more up-tempo and energised than the original.

'Dying Crapshooter's Blues' (Blind Willie McTell)
This Blind Willie McTell song is similar to the better-known 'St. James Infirmary Blues' and 'Streets Of Laredo' in that it describes a dying man's last wishes. Almost a recitation rather than a song, it is a rather bizarre piece. Graham Preskett's piano fills are well executed on McTell's interpretation.

'This'll Bring You Back' (Shade)
McTell's interpretation of this Memphis Jug Band (sometimes called the Carolina Peanut Boys) tune is a fun, rollicking and engaging way to conclude the album. The band is certainly in fine form here!

National Treasure (2002)

Personnel:
Ralph McTell: vocals, guitar
Steve Turner: National guitar
Leah May: backing vocals on 'Hard Times'
Sam May: harmonium on 'Hard Times'
Recorded in Los Angeles, Cornwall and in concert.
Produced by Ralph McTell
UK release date: 2002
Running time: 45:46

Twelve years after his last blues cover album, *National Treasure* finds McTell returning to the genre. In his liner notes, McTell recounts that one of his chief inspirations to record this collection was Blind Boy Fuller's recordings that featured a National resonator guitar. McTell did not purchase a National until well into his career and his love of the instrument's sound inspired the album's name. He explains that the unique sound produced by this model of guitar is due to the spun aluminium cone attached to the instrument's bridge. The cover shows the National guitar he had recently acquired and that features on many of the tracks discussed below. Reviewing the album for *Folk Roots* (August/September 2002), Dave Peabody is full of praise for both the collection and the performer:

> He has such an identifiable quality that whatever he chooses to play always comes out sounding like Ralph McTell. And what a good all-encompassing title *National Treasure* is. National resophonic guitars are definitely treasures; the songs that Ralph has chosen and lovingly covers are also treasures and, of course, after a lifetime of creative songwriting and constant touring, Ralph is a bit of a treasure himself.

'Stagolee' (Trad.)
Often titled 'Stagger Lee', this blues standard has been covered by hundreds of performers and was based on a murder that occurred near Christmastime in St. Louis in 1895. Like nearly every cut on the album, it features McTell's National resonator guitar.

'C'mon In My Kitchen' (Johnson)
This is the fourth Robert Johnson song covered by McTell in his blues renaissance. Though passionate, his take does not sound particularly genuine.

'Saucer And Cup' (Bibb)
If McTell sometimes sounds like he's trying just a bit too hard on numbers like the preceding track, here, he sounds more at home with this softer blues piece written by American Eric Bibb (b. 1951).

'Tickling The Trout' (Mendelssohn/McTell)
Though McTell credits this guitar instrumental to Mendelssohn, this listener believes he meant to acknowledge Franz Schubert, whose 1819 'Trout Quintet' remains his best-known piece. The mistake was corrected when the track was included on the *Sofa Noodling* album.

'National Seven' (Tunbridge)
Here, McTell covers a more obscure original, Alan Tunbridge's ode to a French highway that leads south and thus – as McTell points out in his introduction to this live performance – possibly to three elements of life so appealing to young men: freedom, adventure and romance. The lyric, though, is a sad one, tinged with regret. The narrator must be hoping a change of venue will result in an improved state of affairs. John Renbourn's cover of the tune is also well known.

'Weeping Willow' (Fuller)
A live recording of the tune McTell covered earlier on *Stealin' Back*.

'Hard Times' (Foster)
Bob Dylan delivered a classic cover of this Stephen Foster song ten years before McTell on his *Good As I Been To You* album. This is a May family performance with McTell's daughter Leah contributing lovely backing vocals and son Sam, adding a nice texture via harmonium.

'I'm Satisfied' (Hurt)
Mississippi John Hurt's songs usually leave listeners smiling and this track is no exception. McTell's vocals, supplemental to the finger-picked guitar that dominates the brief piece, reflect a man's peace of mind having found love.

'Pretty Boy Floyd' (Guthrie)
One of Guthrie's Dust Bowl ballads, this song recounts the career of the outlaw Charles Arthur 'Pretty Boy' Floyd (1904-1934), an American Robin Hood figure. Guthrie's romanticised portrayal ignores the fact that Floyd killed numerous men in addition to the deputy sheriff mentioned and deprived many others of hard-earned money via his bank robberies. A mythology grew up around the man because he is supposed to have destroyed mortgages stored in banks. McTell's performance features determined vocals and harmonica breaks. Bob Dylan's cover of the same song is one of the many highlights of the 1988 *A Vision Shared* album.

'If I Had Possession' (Johnson)
This listener finds McTell's cover of the Robert Johnson classic superior to his earlier interpretations of the famous artist's numbers. His guitar work is engaging and his vocals sound more true to himself than on his previous Johnson covers.

'Sweet Jivin' Woman' (Blake)
This is McTell's fifth Blind Blake cover and again finds him in good voice. The woman in question is a good influence on the narrator. Blake's original is titled 'Sweet Jivin' Mama'.

'An Nans Tewl Hyr Dhe'n Mor' (McTell)
In the liner notes, McTell states that the Welsh title of this original instrumental is roughly translated as 'long dark valley to the sea'. More atmospheric than melodic, it is a haunting piece and includes some flourishes that place it in near relation to the blues.

'I Will Do My Last Singing In This Land Somewhere' (Davis)
A beautiful interpretation of one of Reverend Gary Davis's finest compositions that is a perfect fit for the warmth so inherent in McTell's voice. The emotion obvious in the vocal is perhaps partially due to the fact that the track is dedicated to McTell's old friend, the recently deceased Mick 'Henry the Eighth' Bartlett.

'Hard Travelling' (Guthrie)
McTell opts to close the album with an upbeat take on one of Guthrie's most famous songs. His use of guitar harmonics lends a nice touch to what is otherwise a straightforward cover.

Gates Of Eden (2006)

Personnel:
Ralph McTell: guitar, harmonica, vocals
Steve Turner: guitar, bass on 'Gates Of Eden'
Willie Wilson: drums, percussion
Adrian Davis: tuba and sousaphone
Martin Frith: fiddle on 'Song For Woody'
Chris Parkinson: accordion
Nancy March: backing vocals on 'Do Re Mi'
Janet Lewis: backing vocals on 'Do Re Mi'
Recorded on location at Village Hall Stewedios (Cornwall), June-July 2006
Produced by Ralph McTell
UK release date: 2006
Highest chart place: did not chart
Running time: 64:31

This lengthy album is dedicated to Ramblin' Jack Elliott, whose recordings proved so inspirational to the young McTell. Though nearly half the songs are from the pen of the legend Elliott aped, Woody Guthrie, an equal number were written by the man McTell refers to as 'His Bobness'. In *Summer Lightning* (207), McTell expresses his admiration for the Minnesotan:

> I always loved Bob's voice. There was an energy and commitment to the interpretation of his own lyrics and his vocal range is astounding, as he can seamlessly soar from tenor to near falsetto with no crack in the voice as it moves from man to boy. There are hundreds of singers now who have adopted his style based more on Jack Elliott than Woody Guthrie, but essentially, Dylan invented modern rock singing and enabled a large number of people who cannot sing to make it by adopting one or other of his styles.

As a young man, McTell wrote Guthrie a short fan letter. He received a reply from Woody's wife, Marjorie, that simply said: 'Thank you for writing. Keep singing'. It was Guthrie's rambling example that inspired McTell to set out on the road in the early 1960s and it was the compassion Guthrie expressed in songs like 'Pastures Of Plenty' and 'Ludlow Massacre', included here, that served as a template for many of McTell's own empathetic recordings. Indeed, it is compassion that binds Guthrie, Dylan and McTell. This trait is expressed by each performer in songs like 'Deportees', 'The Lonesome Death Of Hattie Carroll' and 'Streets Of London', to name just three examples.

NetRhythms reviewer David Kidman dubs *Gates Of Eden* 'a well-rounded selection that not only captures the essential spirit of Ramblin' Jack but also brings the full range of Ralph's interpretive talents into the spotlight. It's emphatically not just a water-treading album of tired old covers'. Peter

Thaine's cover depicts an image of McTell purposefully striding towards his next gig, guitar in hand, and has become a kind of avatar for the performer.

'Pastures Of Plenty' (Guthrie)
Even though this Guthrie composition is often regarded as a protest song, his recording of it was defiantly upbeat. McTell's reading is slower, more thoughtful and a bit darker, featuring ominous rumblings from the start. It's a fine beginning to the album.

'Vigilante Man' (Guthrie)
McTell's interpretation features some fine electric guitar work from Steve Turner but does not reach the heights of Bruce Springsteen's cover found on the *Vision Shared* album.

'Georgia Bound' (Blake)
On a collection dominated by selections from Guthrie and Dylan, here, McTell finds time to cover a track from one of his other heroes, Blind Blake. Interestingly, McTell includes a verse about forsaking the North for a return to the South and also inserts a chuckle over the dubious prospect of eating possum.

'Do Re Mi' (Guthrie)
Woody Guthrie's lyrics were often quite instructive. Here, he warns would-be emigrants to California that things aren't always what they're cracked up to be and the listener is reminded that misinformation wasn't invented in the 21st century. The tuba work of Adrian Davis is a nice addition to the track, as are the backing vocals. All in all, it is one of McTell's best Guthrie covers.

'Glory Of Love' (Hill)
Though McTell credits this song to Big Bill Broonzy on the album's back sleeve, on the insert, it is correctly identified as being written by Billy Hill. Broonzy's version features a lengthy guitar introduction and is played at a much more upbeat tempo than McTell employs here. Yet McTell's slower pace works to the song's advantage on this strong recording.

'Love Minus Zero' (Dylan)
This Dylan composition was recorded for his transitional *Bringing It All Back Home* album. McTell styles it as a folk track but supplements his reading with some subtle electric guitar accompaniment. Chris Parkinson's accordion adds a further folk layer to the piece.

'Ludlow Massacre' (Guthrie)
A tragic tale of unspeakable cruelty perpetrated in Ludlow, Colorado, in 1914, this lengthy Guthrie composition is lyrically awkward in places but still

quite powerful. As we have seen in our discussion of McTell originals such as 'Water Of Dreams' and 'Bentley And Craig', the bard of Croydon shares Guthrie's hatred of man's inhumanity towards man and injustice. This is a challenging song to sing, but McTell acquits himself well.

'I Belong To The Band' (Davis)
Reverend Gary Davis's composition is a powerful testament to the strong sense of community support and reassurance that comes from being part of a religious congregation. Numerous songs have been written about the related concept of the 'angel band'. Though readers are by now quite familiar with McTell's struggles with faith, as they listen to this track, they detect no irony. Sometimes, McTell genuinely wished he so belonged.

'Gates Of Eden' (Dylan)
This listener finds Dylan's 'Gates Of Eden' pretentious, tedious and overwritten, but he is in the distinct minority. McTell clearly treasures every word and chose to name the album after the 1965 composition. Where the truth lies is clearly outside the gates of Eden.

'About A Spoonful' (Lipscombe)
Not to be confused with Willie Dixon's 'Spoonful' recorded by Howlin' Wolf and numerous rock 'n' rollers, Lipscombe's song describes a hangover and other more general ailments. Willie Wilson's drums and Parkinson's accordion add some pep to the recording.

'You Got To Change Your Mind' (Fuller)
Yet another Blind Boy Fuller interpretation that is as lively and fun as the original.

'Prisoner's River' (Guthrie)
The other Guthrie selections McTell chose for this album are well-known, but this track is much more obscure. While eager to join the likes of Billy Bragg and Wilco as performers recognised for recording Guthrie lyrics never set to music, McTell never got the chance until now. Here, he sets Guthrie's wistful lyrics about deliverance and freedom to a melody that recalls 'Red River Valley' and includes a beautiful guitar solo. A definite highlight of the collection.

'To Ramona' (Dylan)
A no-frills reading of the poetic song included on 1964's *Another Side Of Bob Dylan*.

'One Too Many Mornings' (Dylan)
McTell has expressed his admiration for this piece as a testament to the hopes and challenges of his entire generation. Indeed, it is one of Dylan's best early

compositions and though one may view it simply as a love song, it can also be interpreted as offering a bridge to the generation gap so prevalent in the sixties. McTell's interpretation is understandably reverential.

'Song For Woody' (Dylan)
One of the two original pieces Dylan included on his debut album, its original title is 'Song To Woody'. Besides adjusting the title, McTell includes a few interesting variants here. Appropriately, he substitutes 'Bob wrote you a song' for 'I wrote you this song' and closes the gentle track with lovely fiddle work from Martin Frith. On a collection that contains five selections each from Guthrie and Dylan, the young Minnesotan's paean to the Dust Bowl balladeer is an apt conclusion.

About Time (With Wizz Jones) (2016)

Personnel:
Ralph McTell: guitar, harmonica, vocals
Wizz Jones: guitar, vocals
Recorded at RMS Studios
Produced by Ralph McTell
UK release date: 2016
Highest chart place: did not chart
Running time: 44:21

McTell had long wanted to record an album with his mentor, Raymond Ronald 'Wizz' Jones (b. 1939). McTell (Bean 68): 'I saw Wizz Jones playing on Brighton Beach and I became absolutely devoted to his playing. He was the real article. He plays blues like those old black guys do. He misses bars out and he plays riffs as long as he wants to. He's almost impossible to play with, he just does his own thing'. Despite this last observation, McTell and Jones blend as well as tea and milk on this recording. Their voices complement each other and their understanding of folk and blues numbers sounds entirely natural.

The material they cover is quite varied. Predictably, Guthrie and Dylan are sampled, but so is Townes Van Zandt. Three traditional American folk songs are performed, but a jazz-tinged track is also included, as is a pop cover. More unusual selections include an Amazing Rhythm Aces tune, a Grandpa Jones composition and a number by a good friend of Jones, Alan Tunbridge. Whatever the provenance of the songs, a gentle feel of two old friends enjoying each other's company pervades each recording. The cover illustration by Stephen Ashurst shows McTell looking on admiringly as Jones leans into his guitar part.

Reviewing *About Time* for *Living Tradition*, Frank Bechhofer writes that:

> This album is for everyone, but especially for those who remember Cornwall in the 60s or want to get a sense of what it was like. It isn't perfect, and it wasn't then, but it has a great atmosphere; these guys care about the songs and it is an object lesson in how to put a song across. The playing is varied in style and rock solid.

'Honey Babe Blues' (Trad.)
A country blues classic covered by dozens of performers, including Doc Watson, this piece sets the tone for the album with vocal harmonies, harmonica fills and a dual acoustic guitar attack.

'Out Of The Snow' (Smith)
Jones handles lead vocal duties on this Amazing Rhythm Aces tune. His voice is relaxed and pleasant as he relates a story that any veteran travelling

musician can appreciate: finding a friendly port in the storm during yet another tour.

'You're Gonna Quit Me Baby' (Phelps)
McTell and Jones alternate vocals on this Blind Blake tune, also covered by Bob Dylan on his *Good As I Been To You* album. Dylan's interpretation is grittier than this performance.

'Deportees' (Guthrie)
Woody Guthrie wrote the lyrics to this song after learning of a plane wreck at Los Gatos Canyon that killed 28 migrant workers. Martin Hoffman set Guthrie's words to a lovely melody and the sad tale became a staple in many a folk singer's repertoire. Judy Collins and Joan Baez have both recorded touching interpretations. It is a song of questions to which the listener sadly knows the answers. McTell's vocals are ably assisted by Jones in their firm but emotional rendering.

'You Won't Let Me Go' (Johnson/Allen)
Jones is in fine voice on this cover of a Buddy Johnson (1915-1977) song, originally released in 1941. Johnson played blues piano and had a long career as a bandleader, but the duo's arrangement here is such that it does not sound out of place as a folk number.

'Diamond Joe' (Trad.)
As we have seen, McTell feels a great reverence for Ramblin' Jack Elliott and his version of this traditional selection betrays such admiration. Some claim that the song Elliott sang is not from the tradition at all but was composed by Butch Hawes, Alan Lomax's brother-in-law. In any case, its melody and general tone owe much to 'The State Of Arkansas', an American traditional song beloved and often performed by Lee Hays of Weavers fame.

'Old Rattler's Pup' (Louis Jones)
Louis Jones (1913-1998), the composer of this bouncy piece, was better known as Grandpa Jones. A highly successful musician, Jones found additional fame late in his career when he joined the cast of the popular American television show *Hee Haw*. Jones' instrument of choice was the banjo and here, McTell accompanies his partner with some energetic picking on the instrument now most associated with bluegrass. Credit should be given to the two Englishmen for making this song of the American South sound genuine here.

'If I Needed You' (Van Zandt)
After 'Pancho and Lefty', this is American folk singer Townes Van Zandt's (1944-1997) most covered song. The lyrics exemplify the kind of emotional

support everyone longs for. McTell's and Jones' voices blend nicely on this solid cover.

'Tell Her You Love Her Right Now' (Trad.)
More obscure than most of the other tracks on this album, this number offers a surefire antidote for potential regret.

'Abandoned Love' (Dylan)
A Dylan composition that came to light only via his first official Bootleg release, this song was covered by The Everly Brothers during their comeback. If this version lacks the vocal sweetness of that recording, McTell's solo reading is sure and powerful. He likely heard it sung by the Kentucky duo when he opened for them during a 1987 UK tour.

'When You're Gone' (Tunbridge/Jones/McTell)
Jones originally recorded this Alan Tunbridge song for his 1973 album, *When I Leave Berlin*. Perhaps aided by the emotional weight of the ensuing years, Jones' more recent version excels its predecessor in emotional appeal.

'Morning Blues' (Macon)
Banjo player Uncle Dave Macon (1870-1952) was one of the first stars of America's famed Grand Ole Opry. McTell's tribute to 'The Dixie Dewdrop' includes his own banjo contributions.

'I Never Did Sing You A Love Song' (Nichtern)
The album's closing track was written by Emmy-award-winning composer David Nichtern (b.1948), for Maria Muldaur and was later recorded by Olivia Newton-John. Jones' vocal stylings are obviously quite different from either of these performers but deliver the song's emotional impact more than ably. It is a wonderful way to conclude this enjoyable collaboration between old friends and true professionals.

About Time, Too (With Wizz Jones) (2017)

Personnel:
Ralph McTell: guitar, harmonica, vocals
Wizz Jones: guitar, vocals
Recorded at RMS Studios, spring and summer 2017
Produced by Ralph McTell
Running Time: 46:08

Perhaps the best way to summarise this album is to say, 'same again, please'. It follows much the same pattern as the preceding collection. The cover art is also quite similar, though here, a keen eye can detect that the duo is performing in the famous Cornish folk club, The Mermaid.

'Philadelphia Lawyer' (Guthrie)
McTell and Jones share vocal duties on this clever Guthrie ditty, whose title had become part of the English language long before Guthrie employed it. A 'Philadelphia lawyer' is one quite adept at his practice, but in the song, such cleverness counts for nothing and ultimately costs the would-be lover his life. The economical, understated conclusion shows Guthrie's wit at its best. McTell's harmonica soulfully expresses the lawyer's voice at times throughout the piece. An old friend of McTell's, 'Irish Mick', used to play this song repeatedly, but apparently, the guitarist can't get enough of the tune. Willie Nelson includes a nice cover of it on the notable *A Vision Shared* collection.

'Any Old Time' (Rodgers)
One of the fathers of country music, the singing brakeman Jimmie Rodgers (1897-1933), was famous for including yodels in many of his numbers. Here, Jones wisely eschews the Swiss vocalisation in favour of a more straightforward reading that also does not feature the clarinet, fiddle, trumpet, piano and drums of the 1930 original recording. The result is a pleasant but rather tame interpretation.

'Stealin'' (Trad.)
McTell covered this traditional tune on his 1990 album of blues covers. Thus, it is obviously a favourite, but this version offers little in the way of freshness.

'I'm So Lonesome I Could Cry' (Williams)
Though Williams recorded this famous song in 1949, in his liner notes, McTell says he was inspired to record it after hearing English singer-songwriter Charlie Dore's version. Since Williams was such an expressive singer, covering his songs is risky. McTell's interpretation is well executed but lacks any real edge.

'Shall I Wake You From Your Sleep' (Tunbridge)
Jones knew Tunbridge well and offers a moving reading of this touching song, first covered on his 1969 debut album. Like Johnny Cash, Jones' voice has gained expressiveness over the years. It's a fine recording.

'Long Black Veil' (Dill/Wilkin)
Dozens of performers have tried their hand at this haunting country standard. Though the English performers are in good voice here, Lefty Frizzell's 1959 original is hard to top.

'Old Fashioned Shotgun Wedding' (Tucker Zimmerman)
Jones expresses his admiration for San Franciscan composer Tucker Zimmerman in the liner notes, but the charm of both the original and the cover escapes this listener.

'How Happy I Am' (Incredible String Band)
Though this number is credited to the Incredible String Band, McTell suspects it was written by group member Mike Heron as a secular version of the Reverend Gary Davis song, 'How Happy I Am' (called 'The Blood Of The Lamb' in this album's liner notes). It's a brief, energetic tune that's alluring and serves to energise the collection.

'Louise' (Siebel)
Jones sings this mournful song about the last days of a prostitute. Composer Paul Siebel included it on his 1970 *Woodsmoke And Oranges* album and it has been covered by a wide range of performers, including Linda Ronstadt, Bonnie Raitt and Leo Kottke. Jones writes that Dave Burland's interpretation inspired him to record it. Here, McTell's guitar solo, after the listener learns of Louise's demise, is suitably mournful, while his backing vocals lend just the right level of support. All in all, a fine effort.

'Ghost Riders In The Sky' (Stan Jones)
McTell finds this song awe-inspiring, particularly its 'Faustian morality' (liner notes). His deep baritone is well suited to the gravitas of the piece and Jones's backing vocals are suitably haunting. At times, the Englishmen's attempts to sing American pieces fall a bit flat to this (American) listener's ears, but here they succeed admirably. The song's composer has stated that his vision was heavily influenced by a similar tale he heard from a Native American when he was a boy. Whatever its genesis, it is a powerful piece of music, handled masterfully on this recording.

'Riptide' (Kahn/Donaldson)
The metaphor that is the basis of this song is well conceived. Many a man has been torn between the romance that comes with the possibility of new

love and the keen sense of devotion to one's established – if comparatively less exciting – existing attachment. The guitar solo inserted as the conflict is considered is appropriately contemplative. That no resolution is reached is inevitable and Jones' falsetto final note expresses mild despair.

'Touch Has A Memory' (Atkins/James)
The ensuing track picks up the theme of the power of passion, here, in the form of one of the first senses we develop. Jones' quiet, sensitive reading makes it clear why this piece is one that his listeners request most often at his live performances. Pete Atkin has also recorded a nice version of the song.

'When You've Got A Good Friend' (Johnson)
McTell also covered this Robert Johnson song on *Stealin' Back*. If well executed, this recording does not differ greatly from the previous one. Sung together with Jones, of course, it is an appropriate choice for the collection.

'Best Wishes' (Ashley)
This song's composer, Steve Ashley, is an English contemporary of McTell and Jones. Similar in sentiment to Neil Young's 'Long May You Run' and Bob Dylan's 'Forever Young', it is a tidy and fitting way to conclude the album. Fairport Convention also recorded an admirable version on their 2013 collection, *Sense Of Occasion*.

Compilation and Live Albums

Perhaps the most important function of compilation albums is to introduce listeners unfamiliar with a performer's work to what is generally considered their best or most representative selections. They are, in a sense, forerunners to today's playlists. If some are merely exploitative or unnecessary, others make sense and enjoy great success. The Rolling Stones' collection, *Hot Rocks*, for example, has sold more copies than any of their major studio releases. CCR's *Chronicle* highlights their singles and shows the band at their best. Neil Young's *Decade* includes songs from 1966-76 and satisfies both existing fans and would-be listeners. Sometimes, singles, unreleased or live tracks are included in compilations, all designed to lead the listener to explore an artist's catalogue in more depth. Since McTell had only one breakthrough single, a greatest hits package would have been inappropriate. Instead, the compilations briefly described below mainly fall under the similar category of 'The Best Of'.

McTell's first compilation appeared quite early in his career. His first three albums were recorded for Transatlantic and immediately after his contract with them ended, the label issued a collection in 1970, *Ralph McTell Revisited*, that included the tracks generally considered his strongest. Sensitive, compassionate compositions like 'Clown', 'Factory Girl', 'Streets Of London', 'Michael In The Garden', 'Father Forgive Them' and 'Terminus' are tempered by the fun-loving 'Last Train And Ride' and the upbeat 'Spiral Staircase'. New versions of 'Michael In The Garden,' 'Spiral Staircase' and 'Father Forgive Them' were recorded for the album. Rather curiously, no songs from *Eight Frames A Second* are included.

In the years that followed, the three Transatlantic albums were released together repeatedly (with slight variations) under a number of titles, including, among others, *Streets Of London: The Best Of Ralph Mctell* (1975), *The Best Of Ralph Mctell* (1992), *Definitive Transatlantic Collection* (1997), *Spiral Staircase* (1997), *Streets Of London: The Best Of Ralph Mctell* (2008), *All Things Change: Transatlantic Anthology, 1967-1970* (2017) and *Ralph McTell: Gold* (2021). Such releases reflect both the popularity of his earliest work and the proclivities of the music industry. McTell has been able to acquire most of his back catalogue, but as he told Awde (185), the first three Transatlantic albums represent an exception and are thus 'in every bloody petrol station in the country for a pound each or whatever they are because the first recording of 'Streets Of London' is on one of those'. McTell does acknowledge that this fact keeps his early songs in the public eye and is thus beneficial as well as annoying. A single from 1969, 'Summer Came Along', is included on the *Spiral Staircase* collection. While it is hampered by some throwaway lines like 'time and tide wait for no man that's true', the piece is appealing and its impatient narrator does make a few more original observations, including: 'I'll give you a gold watch to put in the pocket of any scarecrow that you meet'. *All Things Change* is the best of the Transatlantic compilations, thanks in part to David

Wells' thoughtful liner notes and the inclusion of McTell's cover of Leonard Cohen's 'Suzanne'.

Other McTell compilations follow a thematic approach. That is certainly true of *Affairs Of The Heart* (Castle, 1989), a collection of 21 of his original love songs. In 2010, an updated, more extensive set of 56 tracks came out under the same title. Since love is, of course, the most complex of all human emotions, McTell covers a great deal of territory in these compositions. Compassion permeates McTell's entire body of work and is a necessary component of any kind of love. Whether his characters are ageing spouses, youthful lovers or children rising to an occasion that demands great love, they all display varying degrees of compassion. In McTell's hands, these songs become as real as the people we meet every day. They are all examples of McTell's love affair with words, with music, with life. His lyric protestations to the contrary, we somehow cannot believe that there remain many words that this artist cannot say.

While some of his love songs on *Affairs Of The Heart* are fairly conventional ('First Song', 'Nanna's Song', 'One Heart'), many detail separations. These include 'Heron Song', 'If I Don't Get Home', 'One Day Away From You', 'I Don't Think About You', 'Miss You Most Of All', 'Wonderful Country' and 'Terminus'. Five pieces explore Eros or sexual temptation: 'Now This Has Started', 'Sand In Your Shoes', 'The Girl From The Hiring Fair', 'Got To Be With You', 'Dreams Of You' and 'Tequila Sunset'. Perhaps the dominant theme in the collection, however, is longstanding love, especially as it endures in the face of challenges. Songs that illustrate this motif most clearly include 'Bicker And Rue', 'Conundrum Of Time', 'Summer Lightning', 'Seeds Of Heaven', 'Traces', 'I Miss You Most Of All' and 'Naomi'. Finally, McTell presents a few compositions that deal with ludus or the fun/playful side of love: 'In Some Way I Loved You', 'Would I Lie To You', 'Sweet Mystery', 'Take It Easy', 'Summer Girls' and 'Grande Affaire'. In his review for NetRhythms, David Kidman calls the collection 'exhaustive and lovingly sequenced and also refreshingly non-predictable (e.g. no 'Streets Of London')' and concludes with the thought that 'each of the four discs forms a satisfying self-contained programme that's also dutifully complementary to the others'.

To celebrate the 25th anniversary of McTell's first recording, Castle released a 16-track compilation called *Silver Celebration* in 1992 (titled *From Clare To Here: The Songs Of Ralph McTell* in the US). A wonderful collection, and one that introduced the author of this book to McTell's work, it certainly qualifies as a 'Best Of Ralph McTell' album, though such matters are always quite subjective. As a bonus, a track released only as a single previously, 'Stranger To The Season', was included. The song's title originated from McTell's friend, Billy Connolly, who had come across the phrase originally found in Kahlil Gibran's *The Prophet* ('For to be idle is to become a stranger unto the season'). Another possible influence for the song is the American author Studs Terkel (1912-2008), whose writings (including the 1974 book

Working) McTell greatly admired. Always a friend to the working man, McTell performed the song at the 1986 Royal Albert Hall *Concert For Heroes*, a fundraising event for the more than 600 miners who lost their jobs by striking for better working conditions in the previous year. In the lyrics, McTell highlights the emotional toll unemployment brings ('Though we get by on the dole/It feeds the body, starves the soul'), uses both music and seasonal change as metaphors throughout and casts blame on the politicians who have failed to effect change and provide leadership. Reminiscent in some ways of 'Streets Of London', the quality of the gentle track is such that it feels at home sandwiched between classics like 'Hands Of Joseph' and 'Weather The Storm'.

Ralph McTell: The Definitive Collection (Highpoint) appeared in 2008. Standards such as 'The Setting', 'From Clare To Here', 'Bentley And Craig' and, inevitably, 'Streets Of London', are joined by three covers ('Scarborough Fair', 'Stealin' and 'Pretty Boy Floyd'). More recent gems like 'Sand In Your Shoes', 'Peppers And Tomatoes' and 'Easter Lilies' also feature. 'Keeping The Night At Bay', a song McTell wrote for his children, concludes the collection. A number of details familiar to all parents who have tried to put their children to bed appear in the track: the children's insatiable curiosity, a desire to share in the wonders of the adult world and the classic request for a drink of water. The chorus voices adult responses to the youthful pleas, while the final verse includes McTell family details: the name of his youngest son, Billy, and the football club he follows, Fulham. In some ways, then, *The Definitive Collection* is the most wide-ranging of the single album compilations, spanning all periods of the performer's career and including a few rarely anthologised tracks.

Sofa Noodling (2012) is a collection of 14 instrumentals. The title indicates the informality of the recordings, as well as McTell's humility. Talented though he may be, he nonetheless rates himself below the likes of Bert Jansch, Davey Graham and Richard Thompson. McTell eschews picks here, relying on his fingers and nails while playing his Gibson J45. Three of the pieces are included elsewhere ('That'll Do Babe, 'Leah's Favourite' and 'Tickling The Trout'). Four are instrumental versions of McTell originals ('Pity The Boy', 'I'm Not Really Blue', 'Sleepy Time Blues' and a moving performance of 'Still In Dreams'). Three others cover well-known numbers from the past like 'Chattanooga Choo Choo', 'Winding Boy', 'Aura Lee' and the Davey Graham piece made famous by Bert Jansch, 'Anji' (here augmented by 'Lullaby Of Birdland'). The remaining three tracks are McTell originals. The brief 'Barnes Morris' is a melodic and engaging variation of a Morris dance tune originally worked up during McTell's time with the GPs. The up-tempo 'Housewives' Choice' recalls some of McTell's early ragtime pieces. The outstanding recording here, though, is 'John Lee', a powerful, meditative tribute to the great American bluesman, John Lee Hooker (1912-2001), that expertly captures the passion and depth found in his playing.

In 2014, McTell released *Celtic Cousins* (Leola), a collection of 13 songs that have themes related to Scotland, Wales, Ireland and the English county of Cornwall, often regarded as one of the 'Celtic nations'. The Cornish language is similar to Welsh in some ways and was the dominant tongue in this region of England until the area became more Anglicised in the 17th century. McTell's love for Cornwall is well documented and, thus, his inclusion of a live version of the early song, 'Mermaid And The Seagull', and 'Cannabis Creek', warrant a place in this compilation. Wales is represented by 'Nettle Wine', which was composed there, as well as 'Wonderful Country' from McTell's Dylan Thomas album, *The Boy With A Note*.

McTell endeared himself to the Irish population by continuing to perform in Northern Ireland during 'the Troubles'. As noted previously, 'From Clare To Here' has often been mistaken either as a song from the Irish tradition or stemming from an Irish pen. An Irish man, Mr Connaughton, and an Irish nurse who tended to him during his lengthy hospital stay as a boy, were major influences on young McTell. Besides the songs already mentioned above, his love of the Emerald Isle is displayed here via 'An Irish Blessing', 'The Setting', 'The Grey Sea Strand' and 'The Irish Girl'.

Scotland is represented by the environmental protest song 'The Islands', 'The Break Of The Union', and the only previously unreleased track included here, the traditional 'Tangle O' The Isles'. This is a gentle tune well suited to McTell's voice and musical approach. By way of explanation for those unfamiliar with the geography or language of that beautiful region of the world, the Cuillin (or Coolin) Hills are on the Isle of Skye, Tummel and Loch Rannoch are located in Perthshire and Lochaber lies in the western highlands. A Cromack is a shepherd's walking stick and 'tangle' from the song's title refers to seaweed.

2014 marked the 100th anniversary of the start of the First World War. In commemoration of this occasion, McTell released a four-track EP titled *The Unknown Soldier*. His liner notes are lengthy and describe a boyhood fascination with a German officer's helmet shelved in his grandfather's coal shed. Quite how his grandfather came to possess the helmet remains unknown, but McTell became its owner after his grandfather's death. Like most veterans, McTell's grandfather, Albert Henry Moss, preferred not to discuss his wartime experiences. Instead, McTell's fascination with the conflict was heightened by the stories told to him by his Uncle (not by blood relation) Charlie. After appropriately muted, respectful new recordings of the previously released 'The Lamplighter (England 1914 June 28th)' and 'Maginot Waltz', McTell presents two new compositions.

In 'Canopus', McTell gives life to a Cornish legend, the story of a local railroad engine requisitioned for military use in Flanders. McTell begins the reflective song by relating the innocent original purposes of the engine: to transport clay to the sea and to give local children a train ride to the coast annually. McTell's description of the river running white as milk and the sound of singing children pick up the theme of innocence. A brief guitar interlude then serves to conclude the relatively cheerful opening to the piece. The song's fifth verse contains images of opposites: killed soldiers are laid underneath the topsoil, gruesomely illustrating the beginning and end of life (ashes to ashes, dust to dust) and God's original shaping of man from clay to flesh and blood. In the final verse, the ultimate futility of interrupted life is compared to the indifference of the inanimate steam engine, uncaring as to whether its utility is to haul men or clay – in the end, they're the same. McTell has thus invoked the privilege of the poet to reimagine life for his own artistic purposes.

The stately, lengthy title track relates the fate, selection, funeral procession and internment of the Unknown Soldier, as it occurred in England on the 11th day of the 11th month of 1920. McTell speaks the first verse before beginning to sing the composition, whose lyrics successfully stand alone just as well in the form of a poem. The fourth and fifth stanzas are also given as narration to lend the piece appropriate gravitas. If McTell provides much factual detail throughout the performance, his artistry is telling. His description of survivor's guilt as being 'one more enemy to kill' is apt; his observation that 'a bomb does not judge how you played your part/A bullet stops a lion's heart' is rather profound; his recognition of the irony of a bride's bouquet becoming a funereal wreath lends the piece a devastating conclusion. Wisely, McTell keeps the song's accompaniment muted and respectful. The trumpets are gentle, the drums hushed. The author was fortunate enough to witness McTell's performance of the song at his 70th birthday concert at the Royal Albert Hall in 2015.

As Far As I Can Tell (2008), a three-CD set, contains mostly readings of favourite prose passages in chronological order from McTell's two volumes of his autobiography, *Angel Laughter* and *Summer Lightning*, as well as a handful of original poems, a few new versions of old favourites, three previously unreleased songs and four new instrumentals. McTell stitches the prose pieces together by limiting the time between tracks to mere instants and also occasionally includes appropriate sound effects. For those who don't wish to invest time into reading the two volumes of his autobiography, the CDs are instructive.

Two brief instrumentals found nowhere else are included in the collection. 'That Sounds Nice' is a simple harmonica number that follows McTell's narration concerning the purchase of his first Hohner. As the title implies, the very brief 'Fuller And Blake' is a ragtime tribute to Blind Boy Fuller and Arthur Blake. Two songs are unique to the collection. A poetic rumination on time and memory, 'As Far As I Can Tell', is McTell's attempt to come to terms with his life and what its truth might ultimately reveal. The composer's use of light imagery is well rendered in this thoughtful piece, whose title is, of course, rife with double meaning. 'Citroen Light 15' is a spritely, up-tempo song where McTell, accompanied by his banjo, details his obsession with, and eventual acquisition of the titular automobile. Predictably, the dream proves more valuable than reality, as the battered car turns out to be less than road-worthy.

Though released in 2006, it is fitting to conclude our examination of McTell's compilation albums with *The Journey*, a four-CD box set that includes 66 tracks. The collection was the brainchild of David Suff, an artist, record producer and long-time head of Topic Records who had previously completed similar projects for English folk giants Sandy Denny (*A Boxful Of Treasures*), The Watersons (*Mighty River Of Song*), June Tabor (*Always*) and Shirley Collins (*Within Sound*). From start to finish, the project took nearly two years. Suff sifted through 40 years of material, ran his initial selections past McTell and, together, they (along with some help from Nanna May) compiled the final list of tracks. Besides dozens of vintage photographs, the beautifully packaged album includes a handy timeline, a nice tribute to McTell's guitar work by legendary picker John Renbourn, a brief salute from Rory McGrath and a lengthy essay by Paul O. Jenkins.

Reviewers took kindly to the set. Writing for the website *Music OMH*, Helen Wright notes that 'the inclusion of so much previously unreleased material makes this set a lot more than a 'best of' collection. It really is a fitting record of a rich musical career and a must-have for those who already appreciate McTell's talents'. Though he begins his review by admitting that he has sometimes taken McTell for granted, David Kidman of NetRhythms writes that the set 'demonstrates Ralph's artistic consistency over 40 years, as well as charting and following through time the two primary strands of his musical output, the parallel idioms of troubadour song smithery and bluesy raggy re-creations'.

Like most box sets, *The Journey* includes a mixture of live and alternate versions, a few uncollected originals and a healthy number of classic compositions. Nearly half of the tracks appear for the first time. If some are live recordings that differ only slightly from more familiar studio versions, there are surprises and delights aplenty among the other selections.

Previously Unreleased Tracks From The Journey

In 1965, McTell learnt from a friend that he could make his own recordings for only ten pounds at RG Studios in London. In *Summer Lightning* (209), he recalls the hesitation and excitement he felt at the possibility: 'Was I ready to record and, more importantly, did I deserve to record? We used to look at records as a sort of medal of musical achievement back then'. Three of the tracks McTell recorded at RG Studios feature in *The Journey*: Blind Blake's 'Drybone Shuffle', the Welsh mining song. 'The Bells Of Rhymney' and Dylan's 'Girl From The North Country'.

'Girl From The North Country' (Dylan)

In his description of this song in *Summer Lightning* (208), McTell expresses the wonder many have felt at the universality of Dylan's early compositions:

> I was told that he had got the tune from Martin Carthy, but this is only half true. Sure, it does have an English format to it, but it was the ambiguity

of the chords around it and the straight declaration of the sentiment that bowled me over. It was, of course, about Gill (the young woman McTell was then dating). How did he know? How could he have understood every thought and doubt, each regret and uncertainty? How did he know her hair hung long? This was my song; I learnt it straight away.

'The Bells Of Rhymney' (Davies)
McTell's very first recordings reveal a growing command of the 6 and 12-string guitar, enthusiasm and folk sensibilities that are already highly developed. McTell's early vocals, however, still sound a bit unsure, especially on 'The Bells Of Rhymney', a song that indicates his sympathy for miners that later resurfaced in 'The Enemy Within'. In *Summer Lightning* (206), McTell notes its 'beguiling nursery rhyme format as the bells toll out their message. It was a poem written by a Welsh schoolmaster named Idris Davies and underlined, for me, the importance of getting the lyric as near to a poem as possible before you add the tune'. As we have seen, McTell took the lesson to heart in his own compositions.

'Don't Think Twice It's Alright' (Dylan)
McTell's 2006 cover of this Dylan classic shows him in much better voice. The song is a good example of the sense of humour inherent in much of Dylan's early work, a quality that would eventually begin to disappear as the Minnesotan began to take himself more seriously.

'Pasadena' (Trad.)
This track was recorded live at the Folk Cottage in 1967 with McTell's jug band pals, Clive Palmer, Mick Bennett, Bob Strawbridge, Henry Bartlett and a cornet player identified only as Lenny. Though the quality of the recording is poor, the group's brio is worth the price of admission.

'Viola Lee Blues' (Lewis)
Also recorded at the Folk Cottage, this track features Wizz Jones.

'In The Jailhouse Now' (Trad.)
This traditional song gained a new lease on life after being included in the hugely successful soundtrack to the 2000 George Clooney movie *Oh Brother Where Art Thou*. McTell is in fine voice on this live performance in Wales from 2002.

'Ladies Love Outlaws' (Clayton)
That McTell chose to cover this Lee Clayton song (made famous by Waylon Jennings) is another indication of his fascination with American country music. The track stems from the ill-fated 1976 studio sessions produced by Shel Talmy, and while there's nothing particularly wrong with it, the piece does not come off as genuine.

'Marie' (Newman)

McTell opened for Randy Newman in 1971 and has great admiration for the American songwriter whose recordings so aptly recognise human frailties. McTell has indicated his fondness for Newman's *Good Old Boys* album by citing it as one of his five favourite albums. The American's influence on McTell is apparent in compositions like 'Naomi', 'Sylvia' and 'Bicker And Rue'. McTell's cover of Newman's 'Marie', also from the Talmy sessions, finds him in familiar territory and the results are predictably impressive.

'Georgia On My Mind' (Carmichael)

Hoagy Carmichael (1899-1981) was one of McTell's songwriting heroes and a distinct favourite of his mother's. McTell's excellent 1997 studio recording of this standard finds him backed by Richard Thompson, Dave Swarbrick, Gerry Conway and Maartin Allcock, while Christine Collister, Jacqui McShee and Helen Watson supply soothing backing vocals.

'Blues Run The Game' (Frank)

Jackson Frank (1943-1999) was an American singer-songwriter who suffered from mental illness and whose lone album was produced by Paul Simon in 1965. This composition represents his legacy and has been covered by dozens of performers, including McTell contemporaries Sandy Denny (once romantically involved with Frank), John Renbourn and Bert Jansch. Renbourn joined McTell in 1980 on his reading of the song.

'A Leaf Must Fall' (Palmer)

McTell's outstanding interpretation of this Clive Palmer composition stems from the same 1980 session.

'Michelle' (Lennon-McCartney)

McTell contributed this Beatles classic to the 2006 project *Rubber Folk*, a largely acoustic tribute to the classic 1965 album *Rubber Soul*. Both Chris Parkinson's accordion work and the double ukulele attack of McTell and Steve Turner lend a new feel to the song. This is an excellent cover.

McTell Originals Included in The Journey:

If many of these covers are worthy additions to McTell's recorded output, listeners will be most interested in the six original songs that appear here for the first time.

'Alexi' (also spelt as 'Alexei')

This gentle but powerful indictment of the Cold War mentality is exceptional. As in another of McTell's protest songs, 'Peppers And Tomatoes', the narrator identifies himself with the land, characterised here as 'the giver, the taker, receiver of all life'. The Kentucky miners described also make their living from the land. Since they share more similarities than differences with their American counterparts, the narrator wonders why they can't unite as brothers instead of learning to fear each other. After all, the Russian concludes, 'your hands are as dirty as mine'. Coupled with a musical accompaniment that has an appropriately Slavic feel to it, the lyrics are clever and thought-provoking.

'Old Puggy Mearns'

Recorded in McTell's home studio in 2005, this track shows another side of McTell. Based on his encounter with a coal monger, it is a kind of unaccompanied rap that describes, in gruesome and humourous detail, a childhood bogeyman whose father was a sewer rat and whose mother was a mole. There is no real narrative to the piece. It is simply an inventive eight-verse portrait of the kind of man whose role on earth seems limited to terrifying young children.

'Rue De La Montaigne St. Genevieve'

This upbeat outtake from *Sand In Your Shoes* features a woman nearly as intriguing as Mearns, Madame Mattutzi, the manager of a dive hotel on the left bank of Paris. Here, an older McTell looks back on his busking days with both nostalgia and irony. The lines, 'She's a terrible liar I know/But I want to believe her', sum up the artist's particular brand of pragmatic romanticism well. He wants to believe he's walking the same floors once graced by Brigette Bardot, but he knows better.

'A Feather Fell'

This is a live performance of a song later included on a 2010 Derroll Adams tribute album (*Banjoman*). It recounts, in some detail, McTell's 1966 encounter with Adams (1925-2000), the banjo player who had accompanied Jack Elliott on *The Ramblin' Boys* album McTell cut his teeth on. Remarkably, the young man who introduced McTell to one of his musical heroes one day in Brussels was the grandson of the famous Russian painter Marc Chagall. During their encounter, Adams came to life after a few drinks and McTell eventually coaxed him into busking with him. As is often the case in McTell's compositions, there is a great deal to unpack here. One of the few tunes Adams was still capable of playing was 'Little Birdie'. McTell picks up the avian imagery in the fourth verse of the song as he relates how 'a little bird's feather fell that day', a clear reference to his own coming-of-age experience in 1966. Just as young birds moult as they begin to mature, his meeting with Adams McTell represents an important step in his musical evolution, counselled by the seasoned veteran not to try too hard, not to play too loud. The song's final verse reflects the mature McTell's wisdom and again includes the moulting image. McTell ends the piece by stating, 'someone saw a star go out over Portland town', a reference to the fact that Adams was born in Portland, Oregon and that one of his most famous compositions is the antiwar song, 'Portland Town'. Adams' pacifism is picked up by the mention of the dove in the chorus. Though he was in bad shape when McTell met him in 1966, Adams gradually returned to performing and he and McTell remained friends until the banjo man's passing in 2000.

'Messrs. Stephenson And Watt'

McTell is a keen student of history. This song, a gentle, acoustic rumination, is a celebration of the inventors of steam power and lauds their original vision that enabled so many dreams to be fulfilled. The unreleased track from 1982 also includes the romantic notion that the age of steam is not necessarily dead, a theme picked up in McTell's later composition, 'Brighton Belle'.

'Red And Gold'

Best known for its performance by Fairport Convention on their 1988 album that bears its name, 'Red And Gold' is a powerful and personal portrait of the Battle of Cropredy Bridge fought in 1644 during the English Civil War. McTell cleverly links the song's narrator, Daniel Timms (changed through the folk process to Will Timms by Fairport), with the battle by comparing the flower of blood from his self-inflicted wound with the blood spilt by both English armies in the battle. A self-inflicted wound, of course, is an apt metaphor for Civil War. As in so many of his compositions ('Pepper And Tomatoes', 'Another Rain Has Fallen', 'After Rain', 'Alexei'), images of man's fundamental connection to the earth repeatedly occur. The poppy fields, nourished by Englishmen's blood, serve as reminders of both the stubbornness of history and of man's primary relationship with the soil to which he must ultimately return. Though the song is quite long, it is not a tedious listen thanks to its sweet melody and page-turning narrative.

Though McTell's children's pieces lie outside the scope of this book, they are an important part of his creative output. Initially reluctant to move in this direction, McTell recalled that his hero, Woody Guthrie, wrote and recorded many songs for children and, thus, was convinced to take the plunge. Two of his compositions for a younger audience are included in *The Journey*. 'Kenny The Kangaroo' stems from *Alphabet Zoo*, a 1983 Granada television series designed to appeal to children under five. One reason for the popularity of the series, with both children and their parents, is the quality of McTell's compositions. Although many of the song topics and themes were suggested to him by the show's producers, nearly every selection is inventive or engaging in some way and McTell's smooth delivery is ideal for the audience. Kenny, for example, 'boings' about Australia, although he temporarily becomes stuck in the mud. Other quality tracks from *Alphabet Zoo* include 'Albert Ross The Albatross', 'Boris The Bat', 'Gordon The Goat' and 'Holly The Hedgehog', which contains a sly nod to adult listeners in the form of her prickly nature. The other children's song featured in *The Journey* is 'I Like Rubbish' from *Tickle On The Tum*, another children's television series McTell was briefly part of. This raucous number dramatises the old saw that 'one man's junk is another's treasure', or, as we might say today, how discarded items can be repurposed.

In order to establish a McTell canon, as it were, it is useful to compile a list of his most anthologised songs. These include the following: 'Easter Lilies', 'From Clare To Here', 'Love Grows', 'Michael In The Garden', 'Streets Of London', 'Summer Girls', 'Tequila Sunset' and 'The Setting'.

Others that appear on multiple compilations include 'Barges', 'Bentley And Craig', 'Can't Be Satisfied', 'Factory Girl', 'Grande Affaire', 'Hands Of Joseph', 'Keeping The Night At Bay', 'Kew Gardens', 'Let Me Down Easy', 'Mermaid And The Seagull', 'Mr. Connaughton', 'Nanna's Song', 'Peppers And Tomatoes', 'River Rising Moon High', 'Sand In Your Shoes', 'Spiral Staircase', 'Terminus', 'The Ferryman', 'The Girl From The Hiring Fair', 'The Irish Girl', 'Weather The Storm', 'Wonderful Country', 'Would I Lie To You' and 'You Make Me Feel Good'.

Live Albums

McTell is renowned for the quality of his live performances. As he told Awde:

> When an audience and I come together, we work together for an evening because an audience helps, an audience is part of it. I don't want to have everyone get up and dance. Somebody else can do that. But when we all sit down together – or I stand now, but I used to sit to play – and the audience sits there, it's a two-way street. They're the receptors and I'm delivering the thing... It does feel like a celebration when it goes right.

McTell's first live album was released in 1977 and is titled *Ralph, Albert & Sydney* due to the fact that it includes performances from his concerts at the Royal Albert Hall (28 May 1976) and Australia's Sydney Opera House (8 August 1976). To this listener, it remains his best live collection. (The CD release includes five additional selections not on the LP: 'Don't Let Your Deal Go Down', 'Nanna's Song', 'Nettle Wine', 'Lunar Lullaby' and 'River Rising Moon High'). Clocking in at nearly 73 minutes, the CD, in some ways, represents a 'best of' collection and is an excellent introduction to McTell for the uninitiated. Indeed, so familiar are his listeners with many of the tracks that they begin to applaud after hearing their opening bars. Though he would sometimes perform live with backing musicians, McTell is most comfortable as a solo performer. In 2020, he told Awde that when he did perform with others, 'the audience were shouting for the band to leave the stage and to get me back on my own'. The sound quality of the recording is generally good and McTell is in fine form here, including numerous spoken introductions to the songs.

Three jovial original songs appear for the first time on the album. 'Big Tree' is a humorous childhood ditty that recounts the first experiments in human sexuality. One feels even Freud would be amused both by the title of the piece and at the discoveries the children make and McTell himself can't help but chuckle at times during the performance. McTell plays 'Five Knuckle Shuffle' on the piano and even though a few mistakes creep into the performance, it is, nevertheless, an engaging ragtime number that the crowd seems to greatly enjoy. The listener feels as if they are in McTell's living room on a Saturday evening. McTell introduces 'Winnie's Rag' as a 'lovely old Cockney folk song that I wrote', adding that he has not released it to date since its contents might be bad for his image. Indeed, the story is rather salacious (with references to raucous sex and masturbation), but, again, it is infused with high spirits and is an ideal piece for live performance. These songs show another side of a man often perceived by those who don't know him well as 'serious'.

In his review for *Allmusic.com*, Brett Hartenbach characterises the album as 'tender and smart, melancholy and funny', adding his admiration for how McTell is able to 'create a coffeehouse setting in a large concert hall and even more incredible that he's able to evoke that same feeling through a recording'.

Writing for *Folk Roots* (August 1977), Karl Dallas notes that this live album is different from many in that it doesn't display 'sloppy musicianship or a reliance upon phoney audience rapport to convey a sort of instant appeal', adding that it defines the importance of McTell's talent.

Travelling Man, a two-disc live set, appeared in 1999. The recordings from the intimate (295-seat capacity) Purcell Room in London were not originally intended for commercial purposes, but when McTell heard them, he endorsed their release. These are solo pieces with McTell employing his Yamaha L11E and generally find the performer in good voice. All but three of the 25 tracks are McTell originals and span his entire career to date. To this listener, the stand-out selections are 'Gypsy', 'I Don't Think About You', 'Terminus', 'Peppers And Tomatoes' and 'The Ferryman'. Robin Denselow's liner notes stress the artistic range of McTell's compositions and he urges casual listeners to take the opportunity to reassess the performer's entire oeuvre. Rob Beattie reviewed the set for *Q Magazine* in July 1999 and singles out a few for merit: 'Of the newer songs, 'Jesus Wept' is a powerful Dylan-esque meditation, while 'Peppers And Tomatoes' is this decade's 'Red And Gold': a farmer's life, torn apart by war. And few English songwriters can pull off anything as daring as the climactic, Herman Hesse-inspired 'The Ferryman''.

McTell retroactively subtitled this first live album, *Songs for Six Strings, Vol. 1*. Six more volumes in the series followed in the form of six-song EPs, each named after the string numbers of a six-string guitar and contained in the same kind of box that holds strings for the instrument. Recorded between 2011 and 2016, the quality of the recordings is good and McTell sounds at ease with the songs throughout, which span his entire career.

Two songs included in the series had not previously been recorded. 'A Small Voice Calling', McTell's examination of the nagging nature of one's conscience, the 'small voice' of the title, is a fine piece. If conscience is unavoidable, it must not also rule our actions. We need to practice self-forgiveness and find the wine in life along with living the humble life of the meek. 'Things You Wish Yourself' is McTell's holiday season offering originally written for the children's show, *Tickle On The Tum*. McTell's grandchildren, Isabelle and Louis, sing the song with him on this recording, lending it a homey feel. The twist in the piece is that, unlike most pieces associated with giving and thinking of others, it recognises our need to take care of ourselves as well. A hidden track, that includes a humorous backstory to McTell's well-loved children's song, is 'Kenny The Kangaroo' from the *Alphabet Zoo* album.

Suggested McTell Playlists

The Cream of Ralph McTell

'Barges' (*Not Till Tomorrow*)
'Conundrum Of Time' (*Boy With A Note*)
'Easter Lilies' (*Red Sky*)
'England, 1914' (*Spiral Staircase*)
'The Ferryman'(*You Well Meaning Brought Me Here*)
'First Song' (*Not Till Tomorrow*)
'From Clare To Here' (*Right Side Up*)
'Girl From The Hiring Fair' (*Bridge Of Sighs*)
'Hands Of Joseph' (*Water Of Dreams*)
'In The Dreamtime' (*Red Sky*)
'Jesus Wept' (*Sand In Your Shoes*)
'Let Me Down Easy' (*Easy*)
'Love Grows' (*Slide Away The Screen*)
'Maginot Waltz' (*Easy*)
'Michael In The Garden' (*My Side Of Your Window*)
'Mr. Connaughton' (*Bridge Of Sighs*)
'Nanna's Song' (*Eight Frames A Second*)
'Naomi' (*Right Side Up*)
'Peppers And Tomatoes' (*Sand In Your Shoes*)
'The Setting' (*Bridge Of Sighs*)
'Song For Martin' (*Water Of Dreams*)
'Spiral Staircase' (*Spiral Staircase*)
'Streets Of London' (*Spiral Staircase*)
'Summer Lightning' (*Easy*)
'Sylvia' (*Not Till Tomorrow*)
'Tequila Sunset' (*Right Side Up*)
'That'll Do, Babe' (*Stealin' Back*)
'The Girl From The Hiring Fair' (*Bridge Of Sighs*)
'Throw Out A Line And Dream' (*Bridge Of Sighs*)
'Weather The Storm' (*Right Side Up*)
'West Fourth Street And Jones' (*Hill Of Beans*)

Best Love Songs

'Affairs Of The Heart' (*Water Of Dreams*)
'Bicker And Rue' (*Red Sky*)
'Choufleur' (*Bridge Of Sighs*)
'Conundrum Of Time' (*Boy With A Note*)
'First Song' (*Not Till Tomorrow*)
'Girl From The Hiring Fair' (*Bridge Of Sighs*)
'Grande Affaire' (*Streets*)
'I Miss You Most Of All' (*Boy With A Note*)
'In Some Ways I Loved You' (*You Well Meaning Brought Me Here*)

'Let Me Down Easy' (*Easy*)
'Nanna's Song' (*Eight Frames A Second*)
'Naomi' (*Right Side Up*)
'Now This Has Started' (*Red Sky*)
'One Day Away From You' (*Red Sky*)
'Seeds Of Heaven' (*Streets*)
'Sweet Mystery' (*Easy*)
'Tequila Sunset' (*Right Side Up*)
'Terminus' (*Spiral Staircase*)

Songs About Artists and Musicians
'A Feather Fell' (*The Journey*)
'A Kiss In The Rain' (*Somewhere Down The Road*)
'Arthur Blake'(*Blue Skies Black Heroes*)
'Clown' (*My Side Of Your Window*)
'Conundrum Of Time' (*Boy With A Note*)
'Gertrude And Alice' (*Hill Of Beans*)
'Hands Of Joseph' (*Water Of Dreams*)
'Maddy Dances' (*Easy*)
'Revered Thunder' (*Somewhere Down The Road*)
'Sylvia' (*Not Till Tomorrow*)
'The Ghost Of Robert Johnson' (*Somewhere Down The Road*)
'West Fourth Street And Jones' (*Hill Of Beans*)
'Zimmerman Blues' (*Not Till Tomorrow*)

Protest Songs
'Alexei' (*The Journey*)
'Bentley And Craig' (*Water Of Dreams*)
'Blues In More Than 12 Bars' (*My Side Of Your Window*)
'Case Of Otto Schwarzkopf' (*Sand In Your Shoes*)
'Claudia' (*You Well Meaning Brought Me Here*)
'I've Thought About It' (*My Side Of Your Window*)
'Peppers And Tomatoes' (*Sand In Your Shoes*)
'Pick Up A Gun' (*You Well Meaning Brought Me Here*)
'The Enemy Within' (*Sand In Your Shoes*)
'The Islands' (*Sand In Your Shoes*)
'Water Of Dreams' (*Water Of Dreams*)

Intriguing Instrumentals
'An Nans Tewl Hyr Dhe'n Mor' (*National Treasure*)
'Blind Blake's Rag' (*Eight Frames A Second*)
'Dry Bone Shuffle' (*Blue Skies Black Heroes*)
'John Lee' (*Sofa Noodling*)
'Leah's Favourite' (*Blue Skies Black Heroes*)

'The London Apprentice' (*Slide Away The Screen*)
'Rizraklaru' (*Spiral Staircase*)
'Still In Dreams' (*Sofa Noodling*)
'That'll Do, Babe' (*Stealin' Back*)
'Willoughby's Farm' (*Eight Frames A Second*)
'Wino And The Mouse' (*Spiral Staircase*)

Best Blues Covers
'Can't Be Satisfied' (*Blue Skies Black Heroes*)
'Coalman Blues' (*Blue Skies Black Heroes*)
'Fables Ain't Nothing But Doggone Lies' (*Blue Skies Black Heroes*)
'Hesitation Blues' (*Eight Frames A Second*)
'I'm Going To Germany' (*Stealin' Back*)
'Kind Hearted Woman Blues' (*Blue Skies Black Heroes*)
'Louis Collins' (*Blue Skies Black Heroes*)
'Red Apple Juice' (*Streets*)
'Sugar Babe' (*Stealin' Back*)

Notable Covers of 'Streets Of London'
*Endorsed By Mctell
Tony Rice (*Church Street Blues*)
Liam Clancy (*The Dutchman*)
Dana Winner (*Unforgettable Too*)
*Sinead O'Connor (*Thank You For Hearing Me*)
*Mary Hopkin (*Earth Song*)
*Glen Campbell (*Ultimate Live Collection*)
*Harry Belafonte (*Loving You Is Where I Belong*)

Bibliography

Awde, N. *Singer-Songwriters, Volume* 1. (Desert Hearts, 2020).

Bauldie, J. Review of *Sand in Your Shoes. Q Magazine*. n.d.
Review of *Stealin' Back. Q Magazine*. n.d.

Bean, J.P. *Singing from the Floor: A History of British Folk Clubs*. (Faber & Faber, 2014).

Beattie, R. Review of *Easy. Q Magazine*, March 2000.
Review of *Red Sky. Q Magazine*, January 2001.
Review of *Travelling Man. Q Magazine*, July 1999.

Bechhofer, F. Review of *About Time. Living Tradition*. n.d.

Dallas, K. Review of *Ralph, Albert & Sydney. Folk Roots*, August 1977.

Denisoff, R. S. "Protest Movements: Class Consciousness and the Propaganda Song". *The Sociological Quarterly*, Spring, 1968, Vol. 9, No. 2 228-247.

Fitzgibbon, C. *The Life of Dylan Thomas*. (Little, Brown and Company, 1965).

Grenfell, M. *Parallel Lives: The Biographies of Ralph McTell*. (Pomera Press, 2017).

Griffin, S. Review of *Boy With a Note. Q Magazine*. n.d.

Harper, C. *Dazzling Stranger: Bert Jansch and the British Folk and Blues Revival*. (Bloomsbury, 2006).

Hartenback, B. Review of *Right Side Up. Allmusic.com*. n.d.
Review of *Ralph, Albert & Sydney. Allmusic.com*. n.d.

Hesse, H. *Siddhartha*. (Penguin, 2003).

Hockenhull, C. *Streets Of London*. (Northdown, 1997).

Kidman, D. Review of *Red Sky*. NetRhythms. n.d.
Review of *Somewhere Down The Road*. NetRhythms. n.d.
Review of *Gates Of Eden*. NetRhythms. n.d.
Review of *Affairs Of The Heart*. NetRhythms. n.d.
Review of *The Journey*. NetRhythms. n.d.

Kluth, S. Review of *Slide Away The Screen. Record Mirror*.

Leggett, S. Review of Boy With a Note. *Allmusic.com*

McTell, R. *Angel Laughter*. (Maidstone, 2000).
Summer Lightning. (Maidstone, 2002).

Nickson, C. *Review of Easy. Allmusic.com*. n.d.
Review of *Streets. Allmusic.com*. n.d.

Peabody, D. Review of *National Treasure. Folk Roots* (August/September 2002).

Ruhlmann, W. Review of *You Well Meaning Brought Me Here. Allmusic.com*. n.d.
Review of *Not Till Tomorrow. Allmusic.com*. n.d.
Review of *Sand in Your Shoes. Allmusic.com*. n.d.

Unterberger, R. Review of *Spiral Staircase. Allmusic.com*. n.d.

Woods, F.(ed). *The Oxford Book of English Traditional Verse*. (Oxford University Press, 1983).

Woodstra, C. Review of *Slide Away The Screen*. *Allmusic.com*. n.d.
Woosnam, D. Review of *Hill Of Beans*. *Living Tradition*. n.d.
Wright, H. Review of *The Journey*. *Music OMH*. n.d.

Not So Hidden Track: Villanelle for Ralph McTell

Come listen to sagacious Ralph McTell,
He'll lift you up to where you want to go.
His songs catalogue our lives so well.

If the water's deep where Icarus fell,
Then want of pity is our only foe.
Come listen to sagacious Ralph McTell.

In his ears, the blues rang clear as a bell,
And he drew inspiration from their woes.
His songs catalogue our lives so well.

He threw out a line to those under some spell,
Spread seeds of compassion, now ripe to sow
Come listen to sagacious Ralph McTell.

From Paris streets to peaceful English dells
Where barges travel and rivers flow
His songs catalogue our lives so well.

His voice will fill your heart and make it swell,
And, gently, tell you much you ought to know.
Go listen to sagacious Ralph McTell
His songs catalogue our lives so well.

Stackridge - *on track*

every album, every song

Alan Draper
Paperback
128 pages
55 colour photographs
978-1-78951-232-7
£17.99
$24.95

Every album and every song by these folk rock legends.

In the early 1970s, a strange apparition began to appear on the stages of a vibrant UK gig circuit in the shape of a band of West Country troubadours, rejoicing under the odd name of Stackridge. Their music presented an extraordinary mix of styles, containing genres as diverse as folk, classical, progressive rock, jazz, pop and music hall.

Alan Draper traces the ever-diverging and remerging paths of the core four Stackridge songwriters: Andy Davis, James Warren, Mutter Slater and Crun Walter, both within and without Stackridge. It's a trip that spans half a century of recording. Commencing with their eclectic debut album *Stackridge* in 1971, it proceeds via many fascinating musical paths and occasional cul-de-sacs.

The band's 1970s heyday was marked by many personnel reshuffles and after their dissolution in 1976, James Warren and Andy Davis combined to form The Korgis, who scored worldwide hits with 'If I Had You' and the much-covered standard 'Everybody's Got to Learn Sometime'. Also taking in The Korgis, Mutter Slater Band and Davis and Warren solo projects, our trip finally arrives in the 21st century as Stackridge returned for a second career and a heroes' welcome from their dedicated fan base.

Roy Harper - *on track*
every album, every song

Opher Goodwin
Paperback
160 pages
50 colour photographs
978-1-78951-130-6
£14.99
$21.95

Every album and every song by this influential British singer-songwriter.

Roy Harper must be one of Britain's most undervalued rock musicians and songwriters. For over fifty years, he has produced a series of innovative albums of consistently outstanding quality, putting poetry and social commentary to music in a way that extends the boundaries of rock music. His 22 studio albums and 16 live albums, made up of 250 songs, have created a unique body of work.

Roy is a musician's musician. He is lauded by the likes of Dave Gilmour, Ian Anderson, Jimmy Page, Pete Townsend, Joanna Newsom, Fleet Foxes and Kate Bush. Who else could boast that he has had Keith Moon, Jimmy Page, Dave Gilmour, John Paul Jones, Ronnie Lane, Chris Spedding, Bill Bruford and Steve Broughton in his backing band? Notable albums include *Stormcock*, *HQ* and *Bullinamingvase*.

Opher Goodwin, Roy's friend and a fan, guides the reader through every album and song, providing insight into the recording of the songs as well as the times in which they were recorded. As his loyal and often fanatical fans will attest, Roy has produced a series of epic songs and he remains a raging, uncompromising individual.

Bob Dylan 1962-1970 - *on track*

every album, every song

Opher Goodwin
Paperback
144 pages
38 colour photographs
978-1-78951-275-4
£15.99
$22.95

Every album and every song recorded in the formative decade of this famed singer-songwriter.

Bob Dylan is the magician who sprinkled poetic fairy dust onto the popular music of the early sixties. His songwriting sparked a revolution and changed rock music forever.

The diminutive poet/singer claimed he was merely a 'song and dance man', but Dylan altered popular music from intellectually bereft teenage rebellion into a serious adult art form worthy of academic study.

Dylan headed for the sixties as a Little Richard rock 'n' roller but soon turned acoustic folkie. After absorbing the music and words of Woody Guthrie, Robert Johnson and Brecht, he became a vagabond social troubadour. Basking in Rimbaud, he transformed into a poetic symbolist before later immersing himself in lysergic beat surrealism. The chameleon of Dylan in the sixties was bewildering to his followers. His first album was a raw debut folk/blues. He followed this with three acoustic poetic gems, three ground-breaking surreal, electric wonders and four that were more mundane and country-tinged.

But by the mid-sixties, he was a strung-out polka-dotted rock star. He crashed (physically and mentally) before leaving the sixties as a clean-cut country crooner. Dylan had mutated more times than a trilobite. Dylan's ground-breaking music changed the world and his amazing story is revealed by exploring the eleven albums that he released between 1962 and 1970.

On Track series

Allman Brothers Band – Andrew Wild 978-1-78952-252-5
Tori Amos – Lisa Torem 978-1-78952-142-9
Aphex Twin – Beau Waddell 978-1-78952-267-9
Asia – Peter Braidis 978-1-78952-099-6
Badfinger – Robert Day-Webb 978-1-878952-176-4
Barclay James Harvest – Keith and Monica Domone 978-1-78952-067-5
Beck – Arthur Lizie 978-1-78952-258-7
The Beatles – Andrew Wild 978-1-78952-009-5
The Beatles Solo 1969-1980 – Andrew Wild 978-1-78952-030-9
Blue Oyster Cult – Jacob Holm-Lupo 978-1-78952-007-1
Blur – Matt Bishop 978-178952-164-1
Marc Bolan and T.Rex – Peter Gallagher 978-1-78952-124-5
Kate Bush – Bill Thomas 978-1-78952-097-2
Camel – Hamish Kuzminski 978-1-78952-040-8
Captain Beefheart – Opher Goodwin 978-1-78952-235-8
Caravan – Andy Boot 978-1-78952-127-6
Cardiacs – Eric Benac 978-1-78952-131-3
Nick Cave and The Bad Seeds – Dominic Sanderson 978-1-78952-240-2
Eric Clapton Solo – Andrew Wild 978-1-78952-141-2
The Clash – Nick Assirati 978-1-78952-077-4
Elvis Costello and The Attractions – Georg Purvis 978-1-78952-129-0
Crosby, Stills and Nash – Andrew Wild 978-1-78952-039-2
Creedence Clearwater Revival – Tony Thompson 978-178952-237-2
The Damned – Morgan Brown 978-1-78952-136-8
Deep Purple and Rainbow 1968-79 – Steve Pilkington 978-1-78952-002-6
Dire Straits – Andrew Wild 978-1-78952-044-6
The Doors – Tony Thompson 978-1-78952-137-5
Dream Theater – Jordan Blum 978-1-78952-050-7
Eagles – John Van der Kiste 978-1-78952-260-0
Earth, Wind and Fire – Bud Wilkins 978-1-78952-272-3
Electric Light Orchestra – Barry Delve 978-1-78952-152-8
Emerson Lake and Palmer – Mike Goode 978-1-78952-000-2
Fairport Convention – Kevan Furbank 978-1-78952-051-4
Peter Gabriel – Graeme Scarfe 978-1-78952-138-2
Genesis – Stuart MacFarlane 978-1-78952-005-7
Gentle Giant – Gary Steel 978-1-78952-058-3
Gong – Kevan Furbank 978-1-78952-082-8
Green Day – William E. Spevack 978-1-78952-261-7
Hall and Oates – Ian Abrahams 978-1-78952-167-2
Hawkwind – Duncan Harris 978-1-78952-052-1
Peter Hammill – Richard Rees Jones 978-1-78952-163-4
Roy Harper – Opher Goodwin 978-1-78952-130-6

Jimi Hendrix – Emma Stott 978-1-78952-175-7
The Hollies – Andrew Darlington 978-1-78952-159-7
Horslips – Richard James 978-1-78952-263-1
The Human League and The Sheffield Scene –
Andrew Darlington 978-1-78952-186-3
The Incredible String Band – Tim Moon 978-1-78952-107-8
Iron Maiden – Steve Pilkington 978-1-78952-061-3
Joe Jackson – Richard James 978-1-78952-189-4
Jefferson Airplane – Richard Butterworth 978-1-78952-143-6
Jethro Tull – Jordan Blum 978-1-78952-016-3
Elton John in the 1970s – Peter Kearns 978-1-78952-034-7
Billy Joel – Lisa Torem 978-1-78952-183-2
Judas Priest – John Tucker 978-1-78952-018-7
Kansas – Kevin Cummings 978-1-78952-057-6
The Kinks – Martin Hutchinson 978-1-78952-172-6
Korn – Matt Karpe 978-1-78952-153-5
Led Zeppelin – Steve Pilkington 978-1-78952-151-1
Level 42 – Matt Philips 978-1-78952-102-3
Little Feat – Georg Purvis - 978-1-78952-168-9
Aimee Mann – Jez Rowden 978-1-78952-036-1
Joni Mitchell – Peter Kearns 978-1-78952-081-1
The Moody Blues – Geoffrey Feakes 978-1-78952-042-2
Motorhead – Duncan Harris 978-1-78952-173-3
Nektar – Scott Meze – 978-1-78952-257-0
New Order – Dennis Remmer – 978-1-78952-249-5
Nightwish – Simon McMurdo – 978-1-78952-270-9
Laura Nyro – Philip Ward 978-1-78952-182-5
Mike Oldfield – Ryan Yard 978-1-78952-060-6
Opeth – Jordan Blum 978-1-78-952-166-5
Pearl Jam – Ben L. Connor 978-1-78952-188-7
Tom Petty – Richard James 978-1-78952-128-3
Pink Floyd – Richard Butterworth 978-1-78952-242-6
The Police – Pete Braidis 978-1-78952-158-0
Porcupine Tree – Nick Holmes 978-1-78952-144-3
Queen – Andrew Wild 978-1-78952-003-3
Radiohead – William Allen 978-1-78952-149-8
Rancid – Paul Matts 989-1-78952-187-0
Renaissance – David Detmer 978-1-78952-062-0
REO Speedwagon – Jim Romag 978-1-78952-262-4
The Rolling Stones 1963-80 – Steve Pilkington 978-1-78952-017-0
The Smiths and Morrissey – Tommy Gunnarsson 978-1-78952-140-5
Spirit – Rev. Keith A. Gordon – 978-1-78952- 248-8
Stackridge – Alan Draper 978-1-78952-232-7

Status Quo the Frantic Four Years – Richard James 978-1-78952-160-3
Steely Dan – Jez Rowden 978-1-78952-043-9
Steve Hackett – Geoffrey Feakes 978-1-78952-098-9
Tears For Fears – Paul Clark - 978-178952-238-9
Thin Lizzy – Graeme Stroud 978-1-78952-064-4
Tool – Matt Karpe 978-1-78952-234-1
Toto – Jacob Holm-Lupo 978-1-78952-019-4
U2 – Eoghan Lyng 978-1-78952-078-1
UFO – Richard James 978-1-78952-073-6
Van Der Graaf Generator – Dan Coffey 978-1-78952-031-6
Van Halen – Morgan Brown – 9781-78952-256-3
The Who – Geoffrey Feakes 978-1-78952-076-7
Roy Wood and the Move – James R Turner 978-1-78952-008-8
Yes – Stephen Lambe 978-1-78952-001-9
Frank Zappa 1966 to 1979 – Eric Benac 978-1-78952-033-0
Warren Zevon – Peter Gallagher 978-1-78952-170-2
10CC – Peter Kearns 978-1-78952-054-5

Decades Series

The Bee Gees in the 1960s – Andrew Mon Hughes et al 978-1-78952-148-1
The Bee Gees in the 1970s – Andrew Mon Hughes et al 978-1-78952-179-5
Black Sabbath in the 1970s – Chris Sutton 978-1-78952-171-9
Britpop – Peter Richard Adams and Matt Pooler 978-1-78952-169-6
Phil Collins in the 1980s – Andrew Wild 978-1-78952-185-6
Alice Cooper in the 1970s – Chris Sutton 978-1-78952-104-7
Alice Cooper in the 1980s – Chris Sutton 978-1-78952-259-4
Curved Air in the 1970s – Laura Shenton 978-1-78952-069-9
Donovan in the 1960s – Jeff Fitzgerald 978-1-78952-233-4
Bob Dylan in the 1980s – Don Klees 978-1-78952-157-3
Brian Eno in the 1970s – Gary Parsons 978-1-78952-239-6
Faith No More in the 1990s – Matt Karpe 978-1-78952-250-1
Fleetwood Mac in the 1970s – Andrew Wild 978-1-78952-105-4
Fleetwood Mac in the 1980s – Don Klees 978-178952-254-9
Focus in the 1970s – Stephen Lambe 978-1-78952-079-8
Free and Bad Company in the 1970s – John Van der Kiste 978-1-78952-178-8
Genesis in the 1970s – Bill Thomas 978178952-146-7
George Harrison in the 1970s – Eoghan Lyng 978-1-78952-174-0
Kiss in the 1970s – Peter Gallagher 978-1-78952-246-4
Manfred Mann's Earth Band in the 1970s – John Van der Kiste 978178952-243-3
Marillion in the 1980s – Nathaniel Webb 978-1-78952-065-1
Van Morrison in the 1970s – Peter Childs - 978-1-78952-241-9
Mott the Hoople and Ian Hunter in the 1970s –
John Van der Kiste 978-1-78-952-162-7

Pink Floyd In The 1970s – Georg Purvis 978-1-78952-072-9
Suzi Quatro in the 1970s – Darren Johnson 978-1-78952-236-5
Queen in the 1970s – James Griffiths 978-1-78952-265-5
Roxy Music in the 1970s – Dave Thompson 978-1-78952-180-1
Slade in the 1970s – Darren Johnson 978-1-78952-268-6
Status Quo in the 1980s – Greg Harper 978-1-78952-244-0
Tangerine Dream in the 1970s – Stephen Palmer 978-1-78952-161-0
The Sweet in the 1970s – Darren Johnson 978-1-78952-139-9
Uriah Heep in the 1970s – Steve Pilkington 978-1-78952-103-0
Van der Graaf Generator in the 1970s – Steve Pilkington 978-1-78952-245-7
Rick Wakeman in the 1970s – Geoffrey Feakes 978-1-78952-264-8
Yes in the 1980s – Stephen Lambe with David Watkinson 978-1-78952-125-2

On Screen series

Carry On… – Stephen Lambe 978-1-78952-004-0
David Cronenberg – Patrick Chapman 978-1-78952-071-2
Doctor Who: The David Tennant Years – Jamie Hailstone 978-1-78952-066-8
James Bond – Andrew Wild 978-1-78952-010-1
Monty Python – Steve Pilkington 978-1-78952-047-7
Seinfeld Seasons 1 to 5 – Stephen Lambe 978-1-78952-012-5

Other Books

1967: A Year In Psychedelic Rock 978-1-78952-155-9
1970: A Year In Rock – John Van der Kiste 978-1-78952-147-4
1973: The Golden Year of Progressive Rock 978-1-78952-165-8
Babysitting A Band On The Rocks – G.D. Praetorius 978-1-78952-106-1
Eric Clapton Sessions – Andrew Wild 978-1-78952-177-1
Derek Taylor: For Your Radioactive Children –
Andrew Darlington 978-1-78952-038-5
The Golden Road: The Recording History of The Grateful Dead – John Kilbride 978-1-78952-156-6
Iggy and The Stooges On Stage 1967-1974 – Per Nilsen 978-1-78952-101-6
Jon Anderson and the Warriors – the road to Yes –
David Watkinson 978-1-78952-059-0
Magic: The David Paton Story – David Paton 978-1-78952-266-2
Misty: The Music of Johnny Mathis – Jakob Baekgaard 978-1-78952-247-1
Nu Metal: A Definitive Guide – Matt Karpe 978-1-78952-063-7
Tommy Bolin: In and Out of Deep Purple – Laura Shenton 978-1-78952-070-5
Maximum Darkness – Deke Leonard 978-1-78952-048-4
The Twang Dynasty – Deke Leonard 978-1-78952-049-1

and many more to come!

Would you like to write for Sonicbond Publishing?

At Sonicbond Publishing we are always on the look-out for authors, particularly for our two main series:

On Track. Mixing fact with in depth analysis, the On Track series examines the work of a particular musical artist or group. All genres are considered from easy listening and jazz to 60s soul to 90s pop, via rock and metal.

On Screen. This series looks at the world of film and television. Subjects considered include directors, actors and writers, as well as entire television and film series. As with the On Track series, we balance fact with analysis.

While professional writing experience would, of course, be an advantage the most important qualification is to have real enthusiasm and knowledge of your subject. First-time authors are welcomed, but the ability to write well in English is essential.

Sonicbond Publishing has distribution throughout Europe and North America, and all books are also published in E-book form. Authors will be paid a royalty based on sales of their book.

Further details are available from www.sonicbondpublishing.co.uk. To contact us, complete the contact form there or email info@sonicbondpublishing.co.uk